PowerPoint 201
Basic
Student Manual

MOS Edition

PowerPoint 2013: Basic

Chief Executive Officer, Axzo Press:	Ken Wasnock
Series Designer and COO:	Adam A. Wilcox
Vice President, Operations:	Josh Pincus
Director of Publishing Systems Development:	Dan Quackenbush
Writer:	Brandon Heffernan
Keytester:	Cliff Coryea

Trademarks

ILT Series is a trademark of Axzo Press.

Some of the product names and company names used in this book have been used for identification purposes only and may be trademarks or registered trademarks of their respective manufacturers and sellers.

Disclaimer

We reserve the right to revise this publication and make changes from time to time in its content without notice.

ISBN 10: 1-4260-3689-2
ISBN 13: 978-1-4260-3689-7

Printed in the United States of America

1 2 3 4 5 GL 06 05 04 03

Contents

Introduction

After reading this introduction, you will know how to:

A Use ILT Series manuals in general.

B Use prerequisites, a target student description, course objectives, and a skills inventory to properly set your expectations for the course.

C Re-key this course after class.

Topic A: About the manual

ILT Series philosophy

Our manuals facilitate your learning by providing structured interaction with the software itself. While we provide text to explain difficult concepts, the hands-on activities are the focus of our courses. By paying close attention as your instructor leads you through these activities, you will learn the skills and concepts effectively.

We believe strongly in the instructor-led class. During class, focus on your instructor. Our manuals are designed and written to facilitate your interaction with your instructor, and not to call attention to manuals themselves.

We believe in the basic approach of setting expectations, delivering instruction, and providing summary and review afterwards. For this reason, lessons begin with objectives and end with summaries. We also provide overall course objectives and a course summary to provide both an introduction to and closure on the entire course.

Manual components

The manuals contain these major components:

- Table of contents
- Introduction
- Units
- Course summary
- Glossary
- Index

Each element is described below.

Table of contents

The table of contents acts as a learning roadmap.

Introduction

The introduction contains information about our training philosophy and our manual components, features, and conventions. It contains target student, prerequisite, objective, and setup information for the specific course.

Units

Units are the largest structural component of the course content. A unit begins with a title page that lists objectives for each major subdivision, or topic, within the unit. Within each topic, conceptual and explanatory information alternates with hands-on activities. Units conclude with a summary comprising one paragraph for each topic, and an independent practice activity that gives you an opportunity to practice the skills you've learned.

The conceptual information takes the form of text paragraphs, exhibits, lists, and tables. The activities are structured in two columns, one telling you what to do, the other providing explanations, descriptions, and graphics.

Course summary

This section provides a text summary of the entire course. It is useful for providing closure at the end of the course. The course summary also indicates the next course in this series, if there is one, and lists additional resources you might find useful as you continue to learn about the software.

Glossary

The glossary provides definitions for all of the key terms used in this course.

Index

The index at the end of this manual makes it easy for you to find information about a particular software component, feature, or concept.

Manual conventions

We've tried to keep the number of elements and the types of formatting to a minimum in the manuals. This aids in clarity and makes the manuals more classically elegant looking. But there are some conventions and icons you should know about.

Item	Description
Italic text	In conceptual text, indicates a new term or feature.
Bold text	In unit summaries, indicates a key term or concept. In an independent practice activity, indicates an explicit item that you select, choose, or type.
`Code font`	Indicates code or syntax.
`Longer strings of ▶ code will look ▶ like this.`	In the hands-on activities, any code that's too long to fit on a single line is divided into segments by one or more continuation characters (▶). This code should be entered as a continuous string of text.
Select **bold item**	In the left column of hands-on activities, bold sans-serif text indicates an explicit item that you select, choose, or type.
Keycaps like (↵ *ENTER*)	Indicate a key on the keyboard you must press.

Hands-on activities

The hands-on activities are the most important parts of our manuals. They are divided into two primary columns. The "Here's how" column gives short instructions to you about what to do. The "Here's why" column provides explanations, graphics, and clarifications. Here's a sample:

Do it!

A-1: Creating a commission formula

Here's how	Here's why
1 Open Sales	This is an oversimplified sales compensation worksheet. It shows sales totals, commissions, and incentives for five sales reps.
2 Observe the contents of cell F4	F4 ▼ = =E4*C_Rate
	The commission rate formulas use the name "C_Rate" instead of a value for the commission rate.

For these activities, we have provided a collection of data files designed to help you learn each skill in a real-world business context. As you work through the activities, you will modify and update these files. Of course, you might make a mistake and therefore want to re-key the activity starting from scratch. To make it easy to start over, you will rename each data file at the end of the first activity in which the file is modified. Our convention for renaming files is to add the word "My" to the beginning of the file name. In the above activity, for example, a file called "Sales" is being used for the first time. At the end of this activity, you would save the file as "My sales," thus leaving the "Sales" file unchanged. If you make a mistake, you can start over using the original "Sales" file.

In some activities, however, it might not be practical to rename the data file. If you want to retry one of these activities, ask your instructor for a fresh copy of the original data file.

Topic B: Setting your expectations

Properly setting your expectations is essential to your success. This topic will help you do that by providing:

- Prerequisites for this course
- A description of the target student
- A list of the objectives for the course
- A skills assessment for the course

Course prerequisites

Before taking this course, you should be familiar with personal computers and the use of a keyboard and a mouse. Furthermore, this course assumes that you've completed the following course or have equivalent experience:

- *Windows XP: Basic, Windows Vista: Basic,* or *Windows 7: Basic*

Target student

You will get the most out of this course if your goal is to learn the basic features of PowerPoint to create presentations. You will learn how to create and format presentations, apply content and styles, use templates, create shapes, charts, and tables, and prepare their presentations for delivery. You should be comfortable using a personal computer and Microsoft Windows XP or Vista, or preferably Windows 7.

Course objectives

These overall course objectives will give you an idea about what to expect from the course. It is also possible that they will help you see that this course is not the right one for you. If you think you either lack the prerequisite knowledge or already know most of the subject matter to be covered, you should let your instructor know that you think you are misplaced in the class.

Note: In addition to the general objectives listed below, specific Microsoft Office Specialist exam objectives are listed at the beginning of each topic (where applicable).

After completing this course, you will know how to:

- Identify components of the PowerPoint interface, open and run a presentation, switch between views, and control the magnification level.
- Create a basic presentation and add content, arrange, insert and delete slides, and apply templates and design themes.
- Format text and lists, apply font styles, copy formatting, and control alignment and spacing of content on a slide.
- Create and edit shapes, apply shape styles, duplicate and move shapes, resize, rotate, and align shapes, and apply content to shapes.
- Insert and modify WordArt objects, insert and edit pictures, arrange overlapping items, and group items.
- Create and modify tables, apply styles to tables, insert images into tables, create and modify charts, and use SmartArt to create diagrams.
- Proof a presentation for errors; prepare and preview a presentation, hide slides, create speaker notes, use Presenter view, prepare a presentation for printing, and print notes, handouts, and the presentation outline.

Skills inventory

Use the following form to gauge your skill level entering the class. For each skill listed, rate your familiarity from 1 to 5, with five being the most familiar. *This is not a test.* Rather, it is intended to provide you with an idea of where you're starting from at the beginning of class. If you're wholly unfamiliar with all the skills, you might not be ready for the class. If you think you already understand all of the skills, you might need to move on to the next course in the series. In either case, you should let your instructor know as soon as possible.

Skill	1	2	3	4	5
Opening and closing presentations					
Identifying interface components					
Switching between views					
Navigating in a presentation					
Creating basic presentations					
Ensuring backwards compatibility					
Inserting, arranging, and deleting slides					
Inserting, editing, and formatting text					
Saving a presentation					
Inserting slides from other presentations					
Applying templates					
Applying design themes					
Creating and formatting lists					
Formatting text and paragraphs					
Copying formats					
Finding and replacing text					
Copying and pasting text					
Creating and formatting shapes					
Duplicating, deleting, and moving shapes					
Resizing, rotating, and aligning shapes					
Adding text to shapes					

Skill	1	2	3	4	5
Creating and modifying WordArt objects					
Inserting and modifying pictures					
Arranging overlapping items					
Grouping items					
Creating and formatting tables					
Creating and formatting charts and diagrams					
Adding speaker notes					
Hiding slides in a presentation					
Proofing presentations					
Previewing presentations using Presenter view					
Modifying slide size and orientation for printing					
Printing presentations					
Printing handouts, slide notes, and outlines					

Topic C: Re-keying the course

If you have the proper hardware and software, you can re-key this course after class. This section explains what you'll need in order to do so, and how to do it.

Hardware requirements

Your personal computer should have:

- A keyboard and a mouse
- A 1GHz or faster processor
- 256 MB RAM (or higher)
- At least 2GB of available hard drive space after operating system install
- DVD-ROM drive
- A monitor with at least 1024 × 768 resolution

Software requirements

You will also need the following software:

- Windows 7 (You can use Windows XP or Vista, but the screen shots in this course were taken in Windows 7, so your screens will look somewhat different.)
- Microsoft Office 2013 (minimally, you can install only PowerPoint and Excel.)
- A printer driver (An actual printer is not required, but students will not be able to complete the unit titled "Preparing and printing presentations" unless a driver is installed.)

Network requirements

The following network components and connectivity are also required for re-keying this course:

- Internet access, for the following purposes:
  - Downloading the latest critical updates and service packs
  - Downloading templates, accessing clip art from Office.com, and searching for images using the Bing search engine directly from PowerPoint.

Setup instructions to re-key the course

Before you re-key the course, you will need to perform the following steps.

1. Use Windows Update to install all available critical updates and Service Packs.

2. With flat-panel displays, we recommend using the panel's native resolution for best results. Color depth/quality should be set to High (24 bit) or higher.

   Please note that your display settings or resolution might differ from the author's, so your screens might not exactly match the screen shots in this manual.

3. If necessary, reset any Microsoft PowerPoint 2013 defaults that you have changed. If you do not wish to reset the defaults, you can still re-key the course, but some activities might not work exactly as documented.

4. If you have the data disc that came with this manual, locate the Student Data folder on it and copy it to your Windows desktop.

   If you don't have the data disc, you can download the Student Data files for the course:

   a. Connect to http://downloads.logicaloperations.com.
   b. Enter the course title or search by part to locate this course
   c. Click the course title to display a list of available downloads.
      Note: Data Files are located under the Instructor Edition of the course.
   d. Click the link(s) for downloading the Student Data files.
   e. Create a folder named Student Data on the desktop of your computer.
   f. Double-click the downloaded zip file(s) and drag the contents into the Student Data folder.

5. Copy the data files to the Student Data folder, in My Documents.

Unit 1

Getting started

Complete this unit, and you'll know how to:

A Open a presentation, identify PowerPoint interface components, switch between views, and zoom in and out.

Topic A: The PowerPoint interface

This topic covers the following Microsoft Office Specialist exam objectives for PowerPoint 2013.

#	Objective
1.3	**Customize Presentation Options and Views**
1.3.3	Demonstrate how to use views to navigate through a presentation
1.5	**Configure and Present Slideshows**
1.5.6	Navigate within slideshows

Explanation

PowerPoint 2013 is part of the Microsoft Office suite. You can use PowerPoint to create presentations that can combine text, graphics, charts, clip art, and WordArt. The PowerPoint 2013 interface provides easy access to commands so that the process of creating visually appealing presentations is simple and intuitive.

Starting PowerPoint and opening a presentation

To start PowerPoint, click the Start button and choose All Programs, Microsoft Office 2013, PowerPoint 2013. When you start PowerPoint 2013, the start screen is displayed, as shown in Exhibit 1-1.

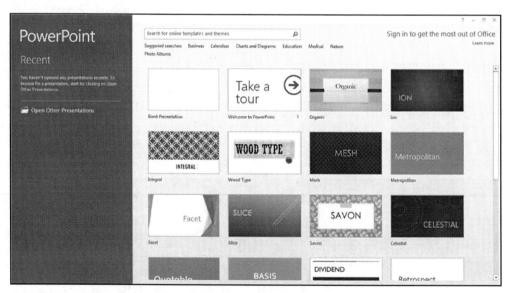

Exhibit 1-1: The PowerPoint start screen

You have the option to select from a list of recently opened files (if any) or start with a pre-designed template or a blank presentation. You can also click Open Other Presentations to go to the Open screen, shown in Exhibit 1-2.

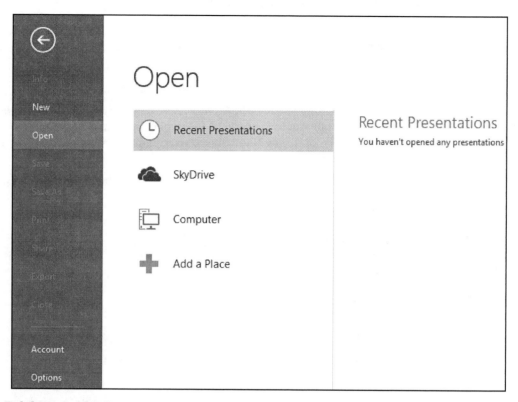

Exhibit 1-2: The Open screen

From this screen, you can open a recent presentation, a presentation located on your SkyDrive (if you have an account), a presentation on your computer, or another network location that you specify. To open a presentation on your computer:

1 From the start screen, click Open Other Presentations.

2 Click Computer.

3 Select the folder that contains the presentation file, or click Browse. The Open dialog box appears.

4 Navigate to the desired folder, if necessary, and select the presentation you want to open.

5 Click Open. The presentation appears in the PowerPoint window and the editing tools and commands are displayed.

Running a presentation

After you open a presentation file, you can start adding text, graphics, and other elements to the presentation slides. When you're ready to present to your audience, you'll run a slide show.

There are several ways to start a slide show. Here's one way:

1   Click the Slide Show tab on the ribbon. The *ribbon* is the panel of options and commands at the top of the application window. It contains tabs organized by function. The Slide Show tab contains commands you can use to start a slide show.

2   Click From Beginning to begin playing the slide show from the first slide.

Moving between slides

When you run a slide show, PowerPoint displays one slide at a time. You can advance the slides manually, or have PowerPoint advance them automatically. To move to the next slide, you can:

- Click the mouse.
- Press the space bar.
- Right-click the current slide and choose Next from the shortcut menu.
- Press the Page Down key. (PG DN on some keyboards.)

To move to the previous slide, you can right-click the current slide and choose Previous, or press the Page Up key (PG UP on some keyboards). To end a slide show, you can press the Escape key (Esc) or right-click the screen and choose End Show.

Do it!

A-1:   Starting PowerPoint and running a presentation

The files for this activity are in Student Data folder **Unit 1\Topic A**.

Here's how	Here's why
1 Click **Start** and choose **All Programs**, **Microsoft Office 2013**, **PowerPoint 2013**	To start PowerPoint.
Observe the start screen	This screen shows several templates you can start with. The orange section on the left side will show recently opened presentations. This section is currently empty but it will change as you open presentation files.
2 Click **Open Other Presentations**	The Open screen appears. From here, you can open a recent presentation, a presentation on your computer, or a presentation on a SkyDrive account or other network location.
3 Click **Computer**	File location options and a Browse button appear to the right.
Click **Browse**	The Open dialog box appears.

4	Navigate to the current topic folder	The files for this activity are in Student Data folder Unit 1\Topic A.
	Select **Outlander Spices**	You'll open this presentation.
	Click **Open**	To open the presentation. The first slide appears in the PowerPoint window.
5	Click the **Slide Show** tab at the top of the window	SLIDE SHOW
		To display the Slide Show controls on the ribbon toolbar.
	In the Start Slide Show group, click **From Beginning**	FILE HOME INSERT DESIGN — From Beginning From Current Slide Present Online Custom Slide Show — Start Slide Show
		To start the slide show from the first slide.
6	Observe the first slide	This is the title slide.
	Click the mouse	To go to the next slide. You'll see a slide titled "Redesign Website."
7	Press (SPACEBAR)	To go to the next slide.
8	Click the mouse again	To view the next slide.
9	Move to the next slide	Click the mouse or press the Space bar. This slide contains a table.
10	Move to the next slide	To view the next slide; it contains a chart.
11	Press (PAGE UP)	To go back to the previous slide. You can use the Page Up and Page Down keys to view all the slides in the presentation.
12	Right-click the slide	To display a shortcut menu.
	Choose **Previous**	To go to the previous slide.
13	Navigate forward to the Website Launch Team slide	This slide shows an organization chart.
	Click the mouse	(Or press the Space bar.) There are no more slides, so the slideshow ends. A black screen is displayed with the message, "End of slide show, click to exit."
14	Click once more	To exit the slide show.

The PowerPoint interface

Explanation

The PowerPoint window has several components that help you interact with the program. Exhibit 1-3 shows some of these components. PowerPoint 2013 uses the ribbon interface introduced in PowerPoint 2007 and includes several enhancements.

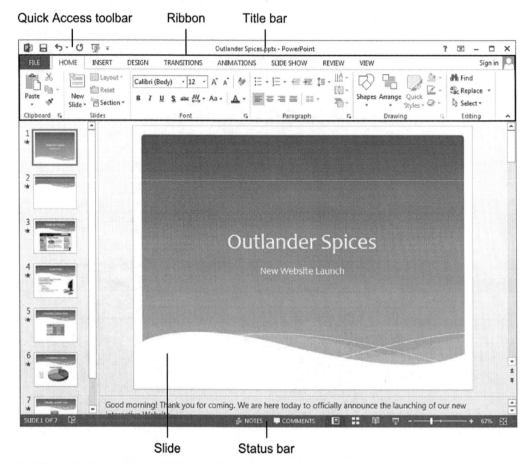

Exhibit 1-3: PowerPoint 2013 interface components

The following table describes the main components of the PowerPoint 2013 window.

Item	Description
Title bar	Displays the name of the current document.
Quick Access toolbar	Contains frequently used commands (by default, Save, Undo, Repeat New Slide, and Start From Beginning). You can customize the buttons on the Quick Access toolbar to suit your preferences.
Ribbon	The main toolbar that contains PowerPoint's primary tools and commands, grouped on tabs named File, Home, Insert, Design, Transitions, Animations, Slide Show, Review, and View. There are also several contextual tabs that appear depending on the actions you take. Each tab contains groups of related commands and options. For example, Exhibit 1-4 shows two ribbon groups named Clipboard and Slides.
Slide	Displays the text and graphics that you create. When you click a text placeholder, a blinking vertical line called an *insertion point* appears. This indicates the location where text will appear as you type.
Status bar	Contains presentation status information, buttons for switching views, and the document zoom slider.

The File tab

In the top left corner of the PowerPoint window there's an orange File tab, shown in Exhibit 1-4. You can click the File tab to access the "Backstage" commands. This is also called the *Backstage view*; it contains the commands you use to take action on a presentation file, including:

- Commands for opening, saving, and closing presentations.
- Commands for displaying file information, opening recently used presentations, using templates to create new presentations, and printing, exporting, and sharing presentations.
- Commands for displaying and editing file properties and options.

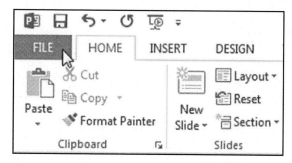

Exhibit 1-4: The File tab on the ribbon toolbar

To open a presentation using the File tab:

1 Click the File tab and then click Open.
2 Click a presentation in the Recent Presentations list to open it, or click Computer to open a file on your computer.
3 Select the folder that contains the presentation file, or click Browse. The Open dialog box appears.
4 Navigate to the desired folder, if necessary. Select the presentation you want to open, and click Open. (Or, double-click the file in the Open dialog box.)

Live Preview

With the *Live Preview* feature, you can quickly view how a different font or design theme will look in your presentation. For example, the Themes gallery on the Design tab displays thumbnails that you can use to see how your presentation will look in a new design theme. All you have to do is point to a theme icon and the current slide will appear with that design theme.

Do it!   **A-2:   Identifying PowerPoint interface components**

Here's how	**Here's why**
1 Locate the title bar	The title bar displays the name of the open presentation (Outlander Spices) and the program name.
2 Locate the ribbon toolbar	(The row of tabs and tools at the top of the program window.) PowerPoint's main tools and commands are grouped in tabs on the ribbon toolbar.
3 Identify the active tab	
Click the **Home** tab	(If necessary, to activate the tab.) The Home tab contains several frequently used commands.
4 Locate the command group names on the Home tab	The Home tab contains the Clipboard, Slides, Font, Paragraph, Drawing, and Editing groups.
5 Click the **Insert** tab	To display the Insert tab's options and tools.
In the Images group, point to **Pictures**, as shown	A ScreenTip appears, describing the functionality of the button.
6 Click the **Design** tab	
In the Themes group, point to one of the theme icons	To see a Live Preview of the theme applied to the current slide.
Point away from the icons in the Themes group	The current slide returns to its original appearance.
7 Activate the Home tab	Click it.

8 Point to the text on the slide   The pointer changes to an I-beam.

   Click the text

                                              To place the insertion point in the text.

9 Locate the Font group   On the Home tab of the ribbon toolbar.

   Click the Dialog Box Launcher, as
   shown

   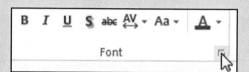

                                              To open the Font dialog box. Some ribbon
                                              groups contain a Dialog Box Launcher in the
                                              bottom-right corner. This opens a dialog box
                                              with additional options and commands.

   Click **Close**, as shown

   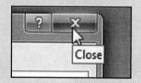

                                              To close the dialog box. You can also click
                                              Cancel to close the dialog box without making
                                              changes.

10 Locate the vertical scrollbar   The vertical scrollbar is a standard interface
                                              component you can use to navigate a file.

    Scroll down   As you scroll down, other slides in the
                                              presentation come into view.

11 Press (HOME)   To return to the first slide in the presentation.

12 Locate the status bar

                                              (At the bottom of the PowerPoint window.) On
                                              the far left, the current and total slide numbers
                                              are displayed. On the right, you can access your
                                              notes, comments, the view buttons, and
                                              magnification controls.

13 Click the **File** tab   The Info page is displayed. This is part of the
                                              Backstage view, where you can take action on
                                              the presentation file. For example, you can
                                              protect the file, view and modify properties, or
                                              share, export, or print the presentation.

14 At the top of the orange bar, click   To go back to the presentation.
    the arrow button

Presentation views

Explanation

You can work in a presentation using any one of five views: Normal, Outline View, Slide Sorter, Notes Page, and Reading view. Depending on your preferences and the tasks you need to perform, you will likely need to switch between views as you work in a presentation. To switch between views, click the View tab. Then, in the Presentations Views group on the ribbon, click the desired view.

View Button	Description
Normal	This is the default view for working in PowerPoint. It displays thumbnails of each slide in the presentation in a separate scrollable pane on the left side of the window. To navigate to a slide, you can click its thumbnail. There's also a notes section at the bottom of the window; you can use this to enter speaker notes for each slide in the presentation.
Outline View	Outline view displays the slide text as an outline. You can use it to organize and storyboard your presentation content.
Slide Sorter	Provides a thumbnail view of all slides in a presentation. You can change the order of the slides in this view by dragging them.
Notes Page	You can use Notes Page view to see your slide and its corresponding notes on one page. This view can be helpful when you need a lot of notes for a slide, or if you want to see how your presentation will look when printed with your notes.
Reading View	Provides a full-screen view of your presentation, just like Slide Show view, but with the status bar and the Windows taskbar visible. This view is helpful when you want to view a presentation on your own or review a draft presentation. From Reading view, you can switch to other views.

You can also use the status bar to switch between views. The status bar displays frequently used views—Normal, Slide Sorter, and Reading View, plus Slide Show, which runs the presentation.

Do it!

A-3: Switching views

Here's how	Here's why
1 Click the **View** tab	To display the view options and tools.
Locate the Presentation Views group	This group contains five view options; Normal, Outline View, Slide Sorter, Notes Page, and Reading View.
2 Click **Outline View**	To view the presentation as an outline. The left pane shows the slide text content. The right pane displays the current slide.
3 Switch to Slide Sorter view	(Click the Slide Sorter button.) The slides appear as thumbnails. You can use this view to rearrange the slides by dragging them into the desired sequence.
4 Switch to Notes Page view	The current slide is displayed along with the presenter notes for the slide. This view is helpful if you want to add a lot of notes, or to see how the slide will look if you print your notes.
5 Switch to Reading view	To run the slide show while showing the status bar and the Windows taskbar.
6 Press (ESC)	To exit the slide show.
7 Return to Normal view	Click the Normal button.
8 Use the status bar to switch to Slide Sorter view	In the status bar at the bottom of the screen, click the Slide Sorter button.
9 Use the status bar to switch to Normal view	

Adjusting magnification

Explanation

Whether you want to see details up close or zoom out to see the big picture, you can easily control your magnification level by using the Zoom controls on the status bar, shown in Exhibit 1-5.

Exhibit 1-5: The Zoom controls

To increase the magnification level of a slide, you can click the Zoom In button (the plus sign), or drag the slider to the right. The small vertical line in the center of the Zoom control represents 100%. You can also click the percentage value to open the Zoom dialog box. In the dialog box, select a zoom percentage and click OK.

To zoom out on a slide, click the Zoom Out button (the minus sign) or drag the slider to the left. You can also use the Zoom dialog box to select to a lower percentage value.

If you want your slide to be optimized to the size of the application window, you can click the "Fit slide to current window" button on the far right side of the status bar.

Closing a presentation and PowerPoint

To close a PowerPoint presentation, click the File tab and then click Close. You might be prompted to save your changes first. You can also press Ctrl+W to close your presentation.

There are two ways you can close the PowerPoint program:

- Click the Close button in the upper-right corner of the application window. If multiple presentations are open, this button closes the active presentation. If one or no files are open, this button closes PowerPoint.
- Press Alt+F4.

Do it!

A-4:   **Controlling the magnification level**

Here's how	Here's why
1 Observe the zoom controls	On the right side of the status bar.
2 Point to the slider	You'll use the slider to zoom out.
Drag to the left	(Without releasing the mouse button.) To decrease the magnification level, making it smaller.
Drag to the right	To increase the magnification level, making it bigger.
3 Click the Zoom Out button twice	(The minus sign to the left of the slider.) To decrease the zoom level by increments of 10%.
4 Click the Zoom In button twice	(The plus sign to the right of the slider.) To increase the zoom level by increments of 10%.
5 Click the percentage value	To open the Zoom dialog box.
Observe the dialog box	You can select a zoom level, or you can enter a value in the Percent box.
Select **33%** and click **OK**	To view the slide at 33%.
6 On the status bar, click ▨	The "Fit slide to current window" button is on the far right side of the status bar.
7 Click the **File** tab	To view the Backstage commands. The Info page is displayed.
8 Click **Close**	(If prompted to save your changes, click No.) To close the presentation.
9 In the upper-right corner of the window, click ☒	To close PowerPoint.

Unit summary: Getting started

Topic A

In this topic, you learned how to open a presentation, **start a slide show**, and go back and forth in a presentation. You explored **Live Preview** and the **Backstage** options, and you identified components of the **PowerPoint interface**. You learned how to switch between the Normal view, Outline view, Slide Sorter, Notes Page, and Reading view, and finally, you learned how to control the magnification by using the **Zoom controls**.

Independent practice activity

In this activity, you'll open a presentation, switch views, change the magnification, and close the presentation.

The files for this activity are in Student Data folder **Unit 1\Unit summary**.

1 Start PowerPoint, if necessary.

2 Open **Training**.

3 Switch to Slide Sorter view.

4 Start a slide show. View each slide, and then end the slide show.

5 In Normal view, change the zoom percentage to 25%.

6 Switch to Outline view.

7 Close the presentation and PowerPoint (you don't need to save changes).

Review questions

1 Name two ways you can quickly start a slide show when you have a presentation file open in PowerPoint.

2 When running a slide show, how can you manually advance slides?

3 When you're running a slide show, which key can you press to end the slide show?

4 Where is the Quick Access toolbar, and what do you use it for?

5 What does the Live Preview feature allow you to do?

6 List the five views you can use to explore a presentation.

Unit 2
Creating presentations

Complete this unit, and you'll know how to:

A Create and save presentations, add content, and insert slides.

B Arrange and delete slides, and insert slides from other presentations.

C Use templates to create presentations, and apply design themes.

Topic A: Creating a basic presentation

This topic covers the following Microsoft Office Specialist exam objectives for PowerPoint 2013.

#	Objective
1.1	**Create a Presentation**
1.1.1	Create blank presentations
1.4	**Configure Presentations to Print or Save**
1.4.7	Maintain backward compatibility
1.5	**Configure and Present Slideshows**
1.5.6	Navigate within slideshows
2.1	**Insert and Format Slides**
2.1.1	Add slide layouts
3.1	**Insert and Format Text**
3.1.5	Create bulleted and numbered lists

Explanation   When you start PowerPoint 2013, the start screen is displayed. From this screen, you can open a presentation from a list of recently opened files, or you can start with a blank presentation file or one of several pre-designed templates.

Starting with a blank presentation

To create a presentation, you can start with an existing presentation and then save it with a new name, or you can start with a pre-designed template or blank presentation file. If you want to create a new presentation from scratch, one that does not contain any content or design elements, you'll start with a blank presentation file. Here's how:

1 Start PowerPoint.
2 Click Blank Presentation. A blank presentation opens consisting of one slide.

Slide layouts

When you start with a blank presentation, the Title Slide layout is used by default. You can apply a different layout from the Layout gallery, which is in the Slides group on the Home tab. There are nine built-in layouts to choose from, as shown in Exhibit 2-1. These layouts are described in the following table.

Layout	Description
Title Slide	This is the default layout for the first slide in a presentation. It contains a title placeholder and a subtitle placeholder.
Title and Content	This is the default layout for new slides in a presentation. It contains a title placeholder and one content placeholder. Type text in the content placeholder, or click an icon to add other types of content, such as tables, charts, or pictures.
Section Header	Contains a text placeholder and a title placeholder.
Two Content	Contains a title placeholder and two content placeholders.
Comparison	Contains a title placeholder and two content placeholders with separate areas for subtitle text.
Title Only	Contains a slide title placeholder.
Blank	This layout is empty.
Content with Caption	Contains three placeholders; a title section and related content section and a content placeholder with icons for inserting different media types.
Picture with Caption	A picture placeholder, along with two text placeholders for adding text to accompany the picture.

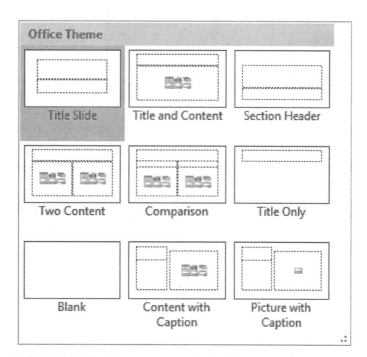

Exhibit 2-1: The layout options in the Layout gallery

Do it! **A-1: Creating a new blank presentation**

Here's how	Here's why
1 Start PowerPoint 2013	Click Start and choose PowerPoint 2013.
2 Click **Blank Presentation**	
3 On the Home tab, in the Slides group, click **Layout**	
	A gallery of layouts appears, as shown in Exhibit 2-1. The Title Slide layout is selected by default.
4 Click **Title and Content**	To view a different slide layout. This layout is slightly different; it contains a title section with a bulleted list and icons for inserting various media types. This is the default layout when you insert new slides.
Open the Layout gallery again	(In the Slides group, click Layout.) The Title and Content theme is selected in the gallery.
Click **Title Slide**	You'll use this slide layout to start a new presentation.

Entering text on slides

Explanation

After you select a slide layout, you can enter text on the slide. The Title Slide layout contains two placeholders for text: one for a title, and one for a subtitle. To enter text, click the placeholder text and begin typing.

Do it!

A-2:   Entering text on a slide

Here's how	Here's why
1 Point to the title placeholder	Click to add title Click to add subtitle
	The pointer changes to an I-beam, indicating that you can add or modify text.
Click the title placeholder text	("Click to add title.") To place the insertion point in the title placeholder.
2 Type **Outlander Spices**	This will be the slide's title.
3 Click the subtitle placeholder text	To place the insertion point.
Type **New Website Launch**	
4 Click anywhere outside the two placeholders	To deselect the placeholder. You can also press the Esc key twice.

Adding and editing slides

Explanation

An effective presentation typically requires multiple slides. To add a slide to a presentation, click the Home tab on the ribbon. Then do either of the following:

- To add a slide with the default layout, click the New Slide button in the Slides group. You can also press Ctrl+M.
- To add a slide with a different layout, click the New Slide menu (below the New Slide button) and then click the desired layout in the gallery.

Adding bulleted text to a slide

The Title and Content layout is the most commonly used slide layout. It has two placeholders: one for the slide title and a second for the content. You can use this layout to add several types of content. One of the most common content types is bulleted text, and the Title and Content layout contains a bulleted text placeholder to make it easy to get started.

To add bulleted text to the content placeholder:

1 Click the bulleted text placeholder.
2 Type the text for the first bullet.
3 Press Enter to display a second bullet.
4 Type the text for the second bullet, and press Enter.
5 Continue this process to add text for additional bullets.
6 When your list is complete, click outside the placeholder to deselect it.

Modifying a slide layout

You can modify a slide layout by formatting, moving, resizing, or deleting its content placeholders.

Deleting text and content placeholders

To delete some of the text in a placeholder, select the text you want to remove and press Delete or Backspace. To delete all text in a placeholder, you can manually select all of the text or click inside the placeholder, press Ctrl+A. and then press Delete or Backspace.

When a placeholder displays only default placeholder text, you can delete it from the slide layout. To select the placeholder, click anywhere on the dotted border, which delineates the boundary of the placeholder. The border will change to a solid line. Then, press Delete or Backspace.

If you delete a placeholder that contains actual text, it will revert to its original placeholder text but the placeholder itself will not be removed from the slide.

Moving and resizing placeholders

You can move a placeholder by dragging it. When you point anywhere on the dotted border that delineates a content placeholder, the pointer changes to a four-headed arrow. Then you can drag the placeholder to a new position on the slide.

You can also change the size of a placeholder. Here's how:

1 Click the dotted border that delineates the placeholder. Squares will appear in each corner and along each edge. These are sizing handles.

2 Point to any sizing handle; the pointer becomes a two-headed arrow.

3 Drag in either direction to resize the placeholder.

Do it!

A-3: Inserting and editing slides

Here's how	Here's why
1 Click the top portion of the New Slide button, as shown	(In the Slides group.) To add a new slide to the presentation.
Observe the new slide	When you add a new slide, the Title and Content layout is applied by default. It contains two placeholders: one for the slide title and another for the content.
Observe the slides pane on the left side of the window	The presentation now contains two slides.
2 Click the title placeholder text	(On the new slide.) To place the insertion point.
Type **Redesign Website**	To set the slide title.
3 Add another new slide	Click the New Slide button.
4 In the title placeholder, type **Launch Plan**	
5 Below the title, click the bulleted text placeholder	(Don't click the icons in the center.) To place the insertion point in the placeholder.

6 Type **Go live next Monday**	To create the first bullet item. The icons for adding other types of content disappear, because by typing, you've specified that this placeholder will contain text, not other content types.
Press (↵ ENTER)	To add a second bullet.
7 Type **Press Kits**	To specify text for the second bullet. The slide now contains a title and two bulleted text items.
8 Triple-click **Press**	To select all the text in this bullet item.
Press (DELETE)	To remove the text from the slide.
9 On the Quick Access toolbar, click as shown	To undo the last step. The bullet point is restored.
10 Point as shown	(Point to the placeholder border, not to a sizing handle.) A four-headed arrow appears at the tip of the pointer.
Click the placeholder border	To select the placeholder.
11 Press (DELETE)	To remove all of the text from the placeholder. The placeholder is still on the slide but it reverts to displaying placeholder text.
12 Select the placeholder again	Point to a border and then click.
Press (DELETE)	To remove the placeholder from the slide.
13 Press (CTRL) + (Z) twice	To undo the last two steps: deleting the placeholder and deleting the text from the placeholder.
14 Select the placeholder	If necessary.
Point to the bottom-left sizing handle, as shown	You'll decrease the height and width of the placeholder. You can use the sizing handles on any of the corners to increase or decrease the height and width simultaneously.

15 Drag up and to the right

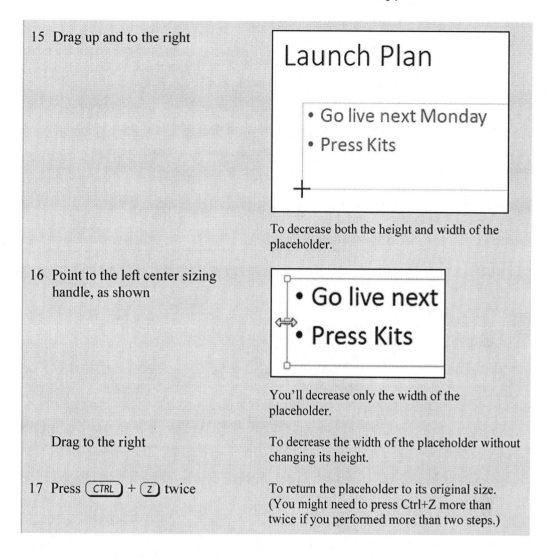

To decrease both the height and width of the placeholder.

16 Point to the left center sizing handle, as shown

You'll decrease only the width of the placeholder.

Drag to the right

To decrease the width of the placeholder without changing its height.

17 Press ⌢CTRL⌣ + ⌢Z⌣ twice

To return the placeholder to its original size. (You might need to press Ctrl+Z more than twice if you performed more than two steps.)

Saving a presentation

Explanation

As you create presentations, it's important to save your work frequently. When you save your file, all your work is stored on your computer for future use.

To save a presentation, you can click the Save button on the Quick Access toolbar or you can press Ctrl+S. When you save a presentation for the first time, the Save As dialog box is displayed so that you can specify a name and storage location for the presentation.

To open the Save As dialog box you can also click the File tab and then click Save As. On the Save As screen, select the desired location. This opens the Save As dialog box. Edit the File name box to name the presentation, and click Save.

Updating a presentation

After you have saved a presentation using the Save As dialog box, you can use the Save command to update your file. This does not open a dialog box because you're simply updating the current file with your latest changes.

To update the presentation, you can do any of the following:

- On the Quick Access toolbar, click the Save button.
- Click the File tab and then click Save.
- Press Ctrl+S.

Do it!

A-4: Saving a new presentation

Here's how	Here's why
1 On the Quick Access toolbar, click 🖫	The Save As screen appears because you haven't named the file yet.
2 Click **Browse**	(The folder icon.) To open the Save As dialog box.
Navigate to the current topic folder	(Unit 2\Topic A.) You'll save your presentation in this folder.
3 Edit the File name box to read **My draft presentation**	To name your new presentation.
Observe the Save as type box	By default, PowerPoint shows the type as PowerPoint Presentation.
Click **Save**	To save the presentation and return to the file.
Observe the title bar	My draft presentation - PowerPoint The file name appears in the title bar.
4 Place the insertion point at the end of the second bullet item	(On the third slide.) You'll add more bullet items to the slide.
5 Press `↵ ENTER`	To add a third bullet item.
6 Type **Advertising**	
Press `↵ ENTER`	
7 Type **Customer e-mail lists**	
Click outside the content placeholder	To deselect it.
8 Press `CTRL` + `S`	To save your changes. You can also click the Save button on the Quick Access toolbar.

Backwards compatibility

Explanation

Since the release of PowerPoint 2007, presentations are saved with the .pptx file extension. Older versions of PowerPoint used the .ppt file extension. If you need to share your presentation with people who have an older version of PowerPoint, you can save it in the older .ppt format. Here's how:

1   On the File tab, click Save As, and then select the folder in which you want to save the presentation.

2   In the Save As dialog box, click the Save as type box. A list of file types appears.

3   Select PowerPoint 97-2003 Presentation.

4   Click Save.

Do it!

A-5:   Ensuring backwards compatibility

Here's how	Here's why
1 On the File tab, click **Save As**	The Save As screen appears.
2 Under Current Folder, click the current topic folder	The Save As dialog box opens. You'll save the presentation in the current folder.
3 Open the Save as type box	(Click it to open it.) A list of several file types appears.
Select **PowerPoint 97-2003 Presentation**	
4 Click **Save**	To save the presentation in a backwards-compatible format.
5 Observe the Title bar	
My draft presentation [Compatibility Mode] - PowerPoint	
	The Title bar shows that this presentation is compatible with older versions of PowerPoint.
6 On the File tab, click **Close**	To close the presentation.

Topic B: Working with slides

This topic covers the following Microsoft Office Specialist exam objectives for PowerPoint 2013.

#	Objective
1.0	**Create a Presentation**
1.1.1	Create blank presentations
1.3	**Customize Presentation Options and Views**
1.3.3	Demonstrate how to use views to navigate through presentations
1.5	**Configure and Present Slideshows**
1.5.6	Navigate within slideshows
2.1	**Insert and Format Slides**
2.1.2	Duplicate existing slides
2.1.4	Delete slides
2.3	**Order and Group Shapes and Slides**
2.3.2	Modify slide order
5.1	**Merge Content from Multiple Presentations**
5.1.2	Reuse slides from other presentations

Explanation

When you're creating a presentation, you might want to change the order of slides or even remove some slides. You can rearrange and remove slides in both Normal view and Slide Sorter view.

Moving slides in Normal view

In Normal view, you can use the Slides pane on the left side of the window to drag slides into a desired sequence. You can also move slides in Normal view by cutting or copying a slide and pasting it.

To cut or copy a slide and paste it in Normal view:

1 In the Slides pane, click a slide icon to select it.
2 On the Home tab, click either the Cut or Copy button.
3 Click above or below a slide thumbnail to indicate the location where you want to paste the slide. A line appears indicating the location the slide will be pasted.
4 Click the Paste button. (You can also press Ctrl+V.)

Do it!

B-1: Arranging slides in Normal view

The files for this activity are in Student Data folder **Unit 2\Topic B**.

Here's how	Here's why
1 Open Website redesign	From the current topic folder.
Save the presentation as **My Website redesign**	In the current topic folder.
2 Observe the slide thumbnails	In the Slides pane, on the left side of the program window.
Click the third thumbnail	To select it. You'll move slide 3 to a new location.
3 Drag the slide 3 thumbnail up above the slide 2 thumbnail	As you drag slide 3 above slide 2, slide 2 moves down one spot.
Release the mouse button	To place the slide in the new position. The slide numbering changes automatically.
4 Press CTRL + S	To save your changes.

Using Slide Sorter view

Explanation

In Slide Sorter view, you can see many slides at the same time, as shown in Exhibit 2-2. You can easily insert, delete, and arrange slides in this view. You can switch to Slide Sorter view by clicking the Slide Sorter button in the status bar. You can arrange slides by dragging them to the desired location in the slide sequence.

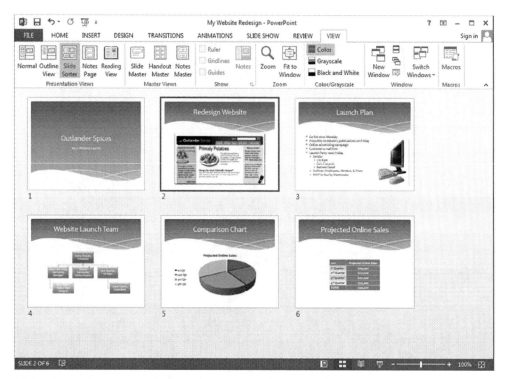

Exhibit 2-2: Slide Sorter view

Do it!

B-2: Arranging slides in Slide Sorter view

Here's how	Here's why
1 In the status bar, click ⊞	To switch to Slide Sorter view.
Observe the screen	This view shows all the slides as thumbnails, making it easy to rearrange slides.
2 Click slide 2	(If it's not already selected.) A border appears around the active slide, as shown in Exhibit 2-2.
3 Select slide 4	(Click it.) You'll move this slide.
Drag slide 4 to the end of the slide sequence	To make it the last slide in the presentation.
Release the mouse	Slide 4 is now slide 6.
4 Move slide 4 to slide 5	Drag slide 4 between slides 5 and 6. The slide numbers update as soon as you release the mouse button.
5 Save the presentation	Click the Save button on the Quick Access toolbar or press Ctrl+S.

Deleting and duplicating slides

In addition to using Normal view and Slide Sorter view to arrange your slides, you can use these views to delete and duplicate slides.

Deleting slides

There are two ways to delete slides in Normal view:

- In the Slides pane, select the slide you want to remove and press Delete.
- In the Slides pane, right-click a slide and choose Delete Slide.

To delete slides in Slide Sorter view, select the slide you want to delete and press Delete, or right-click the slide and choose Delete Slide.

Deleting multiple slides

To delete multiple slides in Slide Sorter view:

1 Select the first slide you want to delete.
2 Do one of the following:

- If the slides you want to delete are sequential, hold the Shift key, and click the last slide you want to remove. The first slide, the last side, and all slides in between are selected.
- If the slides you want to delete are not sequential, hold the Ctrl key and click each slide you want to delete.

3 Press Delete.

The same steps work in Normal view. The only difference is that you select the thumbnail slides in the Slides pane.

Duplicating slides

To duplicate a slide in either Normal view or Slide Sorter view, start by selecting the desired slide. Then do any of the following:

- In the Clipboard group on the Home tab, click the Copy arrow and choose Duplicate.
- Right-click a slide and choose Duplicate Slide.
- Press Ctrl+D.

Do it!

B-3: Deleting and duplicating slides

Here's how	Here's why
1 Select the fifth slide	(In Slide Sorter view.) You'll delete this slide because you determine that your audience doesn't need this information.
2 Press (DELETE)	(Or right-click the slide and choose Delete Slide.) To delete the slide.
Observe the presentation	A line indicates the previous location of the deleted slide. There are now only five slides.
3 Right-click the last slide	
Choose **Delete Slide**	The presentation now contains four slides.
4 Right-click slide 4	You'll duplicate this slide.
Choose **Duplicate Slide**	A copy of slide 4 appears as the new slide 5.
5 Double-click slide 5	The slide opens in Normal view.
6 In the table, select **2014**	(On the slide.) You'll change the year for this slide.
7 Type **2015**	
8 Save and close the presentation	

Reusing slides

You can copy slides from one presentation to another. When you insert a slide from another presentation, by default the inserted slide adopts the design theme of the presentation you insert it into. You can insert slides individually, or you can insert multiple slides simultaneously.

To insert a slide from another presentation:

1 In the Slides group on the Home tab, click New Slide to display the gallery.
2 At the bottom of the gallery, click Reuse Slides to display the Reuse Slides pane on the right side of the application window.
3 In the Reuse Slides pane, click Browse and choose Browse File to open the Browse dialog box.
4 Navigate to the desired folder, select the presentation, and click Open. Each slide in the selected presentation is displayed in the Reuse Slides pane.
5 In the Reuse Slides pane, click a slide to add it to the current presentation.

Changing a slide layout

If you want to use a different layout for a slide, you can apply another layout style. To do so, select the slide. In the Slides group of the Home tab, click the Layout button to display the Layout gallery. Click the desired layout to apply it.

B-4: Inserting slides from another presentation

Here's how	Here's why
1 Create a new blank presentation	On the File tab, click New. Then, click Blank Presentation.
2 Click the title placeholder	You'll enter a title.
Type **Sales Update**	
3 In the subtitle placeholder, type **Corporate Plans**	Click the subtitle placeholder text and type to add the subtitle.
4 In the Slides group on the toolbar, click **New Slide**	(Click the text, not the New Slide icon at the top of the button.) To display the Office Theme gallery.
At the bottom of the gallery, choose **Reuse Slides...**	The Reuse Slides pane appears on the right side of the application window.
5 In the Reuse Slides pane, click **Browse**	You'll navigate to the presentation containing the slides you want to insert.
Choose **Browse File...**	To open the Browse dialog box.

6	Navigate to the current topic folder	
	Select **Website Redesign**	
	Click **Open**	All the slides in the source presentation are displayed in the Reuse Slides pane.
7	Verify that "Keep source formatting" is not selected	(At the bottom of the Reuse Slides pane.) The slides you insert will take on the background and text formats of the current presentation.
8	In the Reuse Slides pane, scroll down to the last slide	
9	Click the last slide	(In the Reuse Slides pane.) To insert this slide as slide 2 in the new presentation.
	Click the "Comparison Chart" slide	To insert this slide as slide 3 in the new presentation.
10	Close the Reuse Slides pane	(Click the X in the right corner of the pane.) You're finished reusing slides from the other presentation.
11	Observe the presentation	The content from the other presentation is the same, but there is no slide formatting because it's based on the blank presentation template.
12	Save the presentation as **My sales update**	In the current topic folder.
	On the File tab, click **Close**	

Topic C: Templates and themes

This topic covers the following Microsoft Office Specialist exam objectives for
PowerPoint 2013.

#	Objective
1.0	**Create a Presentation**
1.1.2	Create presentations using templates
1.2	**Format a Presentation Using Slide Masters**
1.2.7	Modify presentation themes

Explanation

When you create a slide show, you don't have to start with a blank presentation. You
can start with one of several pre-built design templates and then add your own text,
graphics, and other effects to customize the presentation. This way, you can focus on
your content and not spend too much time on the graphics and overall look and feel of
the presentation.

Applying templates

A PowerPoint *template* combines slide layouts, theme colors, font styles, backgrounds,
and sometimes default content that you can use to quickly create engaging presentations
that have a consistent look and feel. For example, if your company prefers that all sales
presentations have the same design, you could choose a template for sales reps to use.

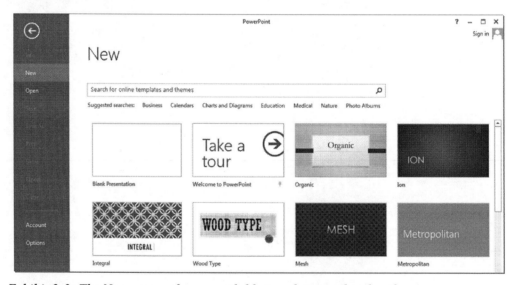

Exhibit 2-3: The New screen shows available templates as thumbnails

To create a presentation based on a template:

1. Click the File tab and then click New. Several templates are displayed, as shown
   in Exhibit 2-3.
2. Click a template thumbnail. You're presented with color variants for the selected
   template. Select the desired option and click Create.
3. Add your presentation content and save the file.

Do it!

C-1: Creating a presentation based on a template

Here's how	Here's why
1 On the File tab, click **New**	To display the templates and themes page shown in Exhibit 2-3.
2 Click **Integral**	A screen appears with color options for this template.
Click **Create**	To start with the default blue theme.
3 Click the title placeholder	
Type **Outlander Spices**	To create a title.
Observe the text	In this template, the title text is uppercase by default.
4 Click the subtitle placeholder	
Type **Sales forecast**	
5 Click **New Slide**	In the Slides group on the toolbar.
Choose **Title and Content**	
6 In the title placeholder, type **2015 sales forecast**	Notice that the new slide also uses uppercase text in its titles. This is because it's part of the same "Integral" template.
7 Save the presentation as **My presentation**	Save the presentation in Student Data folder Unit 2\Topic C.
Close the presentation	On the File tab, click Close.

Applying themes

Explanation

By using a template to create a presentation, you can quickly give your slides a professional look and feel. You can also apply themes to create presentations that are formatted professionally and consistently. *Themes* are collections of shapes, colors, and font styles that you can quickly apply to your slides. You can also apply themes to specific content elements such as tables, shapes, and charts.

To apply a design theme to a presentation:

1 Click the Design tab.

2 In the Themes group (shown in Exhibit 2-4), point to a theme to see the Live Preview applied to the selected slide. To open the gallery and see more themes, click the More button in the lower-right corner of the Themes group.

3 Click a theme to apply it.

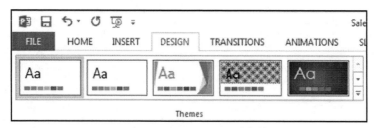

Exhibit 2-4: The Themes group on the Design tab

Using multiple themes in a single presentation

You can apply a theme to an entire presentation or to specific slides. To apply multiple themes in a presentation:

1 In Slide Sorter view or Normal view, select the slides to which you want to apply a different theme.

2 Click the Design tab.

3 In the Themes group, right-click the desired theme and choose Apply to Selected Slides.

Do it!

C-2: Applying design themes

The files for this activity are in Student Data folder **Unit 2\Topic C**.

Here's how	Here's why
1 Open Sales forecast	(From the current topic folder.) This short presentation uses default styles. You'll apply a design theme.
Save the presentation as **My Sales forecast**	In the current topic folder.
2 Click the **Design** tab	
3 In the Themes group, click as shown	
	(The More button.) To display the Themes gallery. Themes are shown in alphabetical order.
Point to a few different theme icons	When you point to a theme icon, Live Preview shows how that theme will look on the current slide. This can help you to quickly find the right theme for your presentation.
4 Click the last theme icon	(The "Wood Type" theme.) The theme is applied to all the slides in the presentation.
5 Observe the other slides	(Click them to view them in detail.) The theme colors are applied to the table and the chart automatically.
6 Select the second slide	(If necessary.) You'll apply a different design template to this slide only.
7 In the Themes group, right-click a theme with a black background	A shortcut menu appears.
Choose **Apply to Selected Slides**	To apply this theme to the selected slide.
8 Observe the slide	The slide uses a different theme from the other slides in the presentation. You might want to do this if you want a slide to be distinguished in some way.
9 Press CTRL + Z	To undo the theme change.
10 Save and close the presentation	

Unit summary: Creating presentations

Topic A   In this topic, you learned how to create a new, blank presentation and apply different **slide layout options**. Then you learned how to **add slides** to the presentation, **enter text** and **bulleted text** on a slide, and edit text on a slide. You learned how to move, resize, and delete **content placeholders**, **save** and update a presentation, and ensure **backwards compatibility** for older versions of PowerPoint.

Topic B   In this topic, you learned how to **arrange slides** in both Normal view and Slide Sorter view. You also learned how to **delete** and **duplicate** slides, and **reuse slides** from other presentations.

Topic C   In this topic, you learned how to create a presentation based on a **template**, and you learned how to apply **design themes** to a presentation or individual slides to quickly change the look and feel of the presentation.

Independent practice activity

In this activity, you'll create a presentation, add slides and text, rearrange slides, and save the presentation.

The files for this activity are in Student Data folder **Unit 2\Unit summary**.

1　Create a new, blank presentation.

2　On the title slide, enter **My Company** as the title.

3　Using the Title and Content slide layout, add a new slide. Enter **New Locations In Major US Cities** as the title. Enter **New York**, **Los Angeles**, and **Dallas** as a bulleted list.

4　Save the presentation as **My practice presentation** in the Unit summary folder.

5　Add another Title and Content slide, and enter **Current Locations in Major US Cities** as the title. Enter **Chicago**, **Miami**, and **Las Vegas** as a bulleted list.

6　In Slide Sorter view, move slide 3 before slide 2, and save the presentation.

7　Apply a new theme of your choice to the presentation.

8　Apply a different theme to the title slide only.

9　Save and close the presentation.

Review questions

1 How do you enter text on a title slide?

2 To add a slide with the default layout to a presentation, you click the Home tab and then click which button in the Slides group?

3 True or false? If you select a placeholder that contains actual text, and then press Delete, the placeholder itself will be removed from the slide.

4 True or false? A theme must be applied to an entire presentation.

5 True or false? All available themes and templates are installed on your computer when you install PowerPoint.

6 To delete some text in a placeholder, you first select the text you want to remove. Then what do you do?

7 To save a copy of a presentation, what command do you use?

8 How can you delete slides in Slide Sorter view?

9 When you're inserting slides from another presentation, what task pane do you use?

10 How can you apply a different layout to an existing slide?

Unit 3
Editing slide content

Complete this unit, and you'll know how to:

A Apply basic text formatting, modify font styles, use the Format Painter, create and format lists, and format paragraphs.

B Replace, move, and copy text, and use the Clipboard pane to manage copied items.

Topic A: Formatting text

This topic covers the following Microsoft Office Specialist exam objectives for PowerPoint 2013.

#	Objective
3.1	**Insert and Format Text**
3.1.4	Apply formatting and styles to text
3.1.5	Create bulleted and numbered lists

Basic text formatting

Explanation

After you add text to a slide, you can select the text and apply formatting to it. You can use the buttons and options in the Font group on the Home tab, or you can use the Mini toolbar. The Font group, shown on the left in Exhibit 3-1, includes the Font and Font Size lists, various buttons, and the Dialog Box Launcher (in the bottom-right corner). The buttons include Bold, Italic, Underline, and Text Shadow.

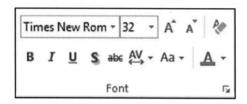 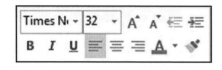

Exhibit 3-1: The Font group on the ribbon toolbar (left) and the Mini toolbar (right)

The *Mini toolbar*, shown on the right in Exhibit 3-1, is a floating toolbar that appears when you select text on a slide. It provides quick access to some of the most frequently used formatting options from the Font and Paragraph groups. The Mini toolbar disappears if you move the pointer away from it after making a selection. You can open the Mini toolbar at any time by right-clicking the selected text.

Selecting text

You can use several techniques to select text on PowerPoint slides, as described in the following table.

Technique	Description
Drag across text	Point next to the first word you want to select, and drag across one or more words to select them. You can also drag in reverse to select a range of text.
Double-click a word	Click a word twice, without moving the pointer, to select the word.
Triple-click a word	Click a word three times to select the entire paragraph or line of text.
Press Ctrl+A	Click within a text placeholder to place the insertion point and then press Ctrl+A to select all of the text in the placeholder.
Shift+click	Place the insertion point where you want to begin the selection. Then point to where you want to end the selection, press Shift, and click. The text between the two locations is selected.

Do it!   ## A-1: Applying bold and italic formatting

The files for this activity are in Student Data folder **Unit 3\Topic A**.

Here's how	Here's why
1 Open Project phase one	(From the current topic folder.) You'll format the text in this presentation.
Save the presentation as **My project phase one**	
2 In the status bar, click [icon]	(If necessary.) To fit the slide into current window size.
3 Double-click **Outlander**	(In the title placeholder.) To select the word. You'll format the title of the first slide.
4 In the Font group, click [B]	(On the Home tab.) To apply bold formatting to the selected word.
5 Select **Spices**	Double-click the word, but don't move the mouse pointer.
Observe the selection	A floating toolbar appears near the selection. This is called the Mini toolbar.
Click the **Bold** button, as shown	
	To apply bold formatting to the selection. Depending on your development preferences, you can use the Mini toolbar to apply basic formatting or you can use the tools on the ribbon toolbar.
6 Triple-click **Project**	(In the subtitle placeholder.) To select all three words in the subtitle. You'll italicize this text.
On the Mini toolbar, click [I]	(The Italic button.) To italicize the text.
7 Save the presentation	

Modifying fonts, font size, and text color

Explanation

In addition to applying bold and italic formatting, you can format text by specifying a different font, font size, and color.

To change the font:

1 Select the text.

2 In the Font group on the Home tab, or the Mini toolbar, click the arrow next to the current font name to open the font list.

3 Point to a font name; Live Preview shows how the font will appear on the slide.

4 When you decide which font you want, click the font name to apply it.

To set the font size:

1 Select the text.

2 In the Font group on the Home tab, or the Mini toolbar, click the arrow next to the current font size value to open the font size list.

3 Point to a font size; Live Preview shows how that font size will appear on the slide when applied to the selected text.

4 Select the font size you want to apply.

To change text color, first select the text. Then, in the Font group or on the Mini toolbar, click the Font Color arrow to display the Font Color gallery. When you select a color, it's applied to the selected text and the gallery closes. Also, the line at the bottom of the Font Color button displays the color you just applied. You can apply the indicated color to additional text by clicking the button.

Do it!

A-2: Changing the font, font size, and color

Here's how	Here's why
1 Triple-click **Outlander**	To select the text "Outlander Spices." You'll make the title larger.
2 In the Font group, click as shown	
	To display a list of fonts.
Point to a font	Live Preview shows how each font will look when applied to the selected text.
Select **Arial Black**	To change the font.
3 Select **Project phase one**	Triple-click any word in the subtitle text.
From the Font list, select **Arial**	To apply the font to the selected text.

4 In the Font group, click the **Font Size** arrow, as shown	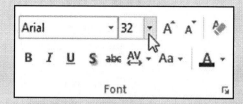
	To display the font size list.
Select **40**	To increase the size of the subtitle text.
5 Go to slide 2	(In the Slides pane, click the thumbnail for the second slide.) You'll format the slide title.
6 Apply the font **Arial Black** and a font size of **54** to the slide title	Triple-click the slide title text to select it, and use the Font list and Font Size list in the Font group.
7 Verify that **Outlander Spices** is selected	
8 Click the **Font Color** arrow, as shown	
	(In the Font group on the Home tab or on the Mini toolbar.) To display the Font Color gallery.
Under Theme Colors, click a light blue square	To apply the color to the selected text and close the gallery.
9 Deselect the text	The text color has changed from the default black to the color you applied.
Observe the Font Color button	The button now shows the last color you selected. You can click the button to apply that color without opening the color gallery.
10 Go to slide 1	
11 Select **Outlander Spices**	
In the Font group, click	(Click the Font Color button, not the arrow.) To apply the same color you used most recently.
12 Save the presentation	

The Format Painter

Explanation

You can use the Format Painter to apply several formats simultaneously. The Format Painter copies all the formatting applied the selected text. You can apply the formatting to other text simply by selecting the text. This can save you time because it reduces the number of steps required to apply consistent formatting to multiple slides.

To format text by using the Format Painter:

1 Select the text that contains the formatting you want to copy.

2 Click the Format Painter button (in the Clipboard group or on the Mini toolbar). The pointer changes to a paint brush icon, indicating that the pointer is "loaded" with the copied formats and ready to use.

3 Select the text to which you want to apply the formatting.

Using the Format Painter multiple times

If you want apply multiple formats to multiple locations, you can double-click the Format Painter button. This way, you can use the Format Painter to copy formatting several times. When you're done, you can turn off the Format Painter by clicking the Format Painter button again, or by pressing the Escape (Esc) key.

Do it!

A-3: Copying and applying multiple formats

Here's how	Here's why
1 Go to slide 2	
2 Select **Outlander Spices**	The title of the slide.
3 In the Clipboard group, click [✎ Format Painter]	You'll apply the formatting of this text to the text on another slide.
4 Observe the pointer	The mouse pointer has changed to an I-beam with a paintbrush next to it, indicating that the pointer is "loaded" with the copied formats and ready to use.
5 Press [PAGE DOWN]	To move to slide 3.
6 Point to the beginning of the word **Project**	(On the third slide.) You'll drag across the text that you want to format.
Drag to select the words **Project justification**	To apply the copied formatting.

7	Observe the selected text	The formatting from the other slide is applied to the selected text.
	Observe the pointer	It has returned to its normal state, indicating that the Format Painter is no longer active.
	Deselect the text	
8	Select **Project justification**	You'll access the Format Painter from the Mini toolbar this time.
	Double-click	(On the Mini toolbar.) To load the Format Painter for multiple applications. You'll apply the formatting of the selected text to the title text on multiple slides.
9	Go to slide 4	
	Select **Cost of expansion**	(Drag across the text.) To apply the formatting.
	Observe the pointer	This time, the paintbrush icon remains active, indicating the Format Painter is still loaded for multiple applications.
	Observe the Format Painter button	The button is also selected to indicate that it's active.
10	Apply the formatting to the title text on the remaining slides	
11	Click **Format Painter**	(In the Clipboard group or on the Mini toolbar.) To turn off the Format Painter.
12	Save the presentation	

Bullet styles for list items

Explanation

You can change the default bullet styles to better suit the purpose of your content. First, select the text next to the bullet (or bullets) that you want to change. Then, in the Paragraph group or on the Mini toolbar, click the arrow on the Bullets button to open the Bullets gallery. Click a bullet style to apply it to your selected text.

If you want to indent list items to create a sub-list, select the items and then either press Tab, or click the Increase List Level button in the Paragraph group

By default, when you indent list items into a sub-list, the text size is reduced and the bullet character changes. When you create a sub-list for a numbered list, the text size is reduced and the numbering re-starts at 1.

You can also "promote" bulleted or numbered list items to a higher level. First select the text and then either press Shift+Tab, or click the Decrease List Level button in the Paragraph group.

Do it!

A-4:   Modifying bullet styles

Here's how	Here's why
1 Go to slide 2	
2 Select the text as shown	 (Point to the left of "Project" and drag down and to the right.) You'll change the bullet style.
3 In the Paragraph group, click the **Bullets** arrow, as shown	 (Or use the Mini toolbar.) To display the Bullets gallery.
Observe the gallery	The current bullet style is selected by default.

4 Select the Checkmark Bullets
   style, as shown

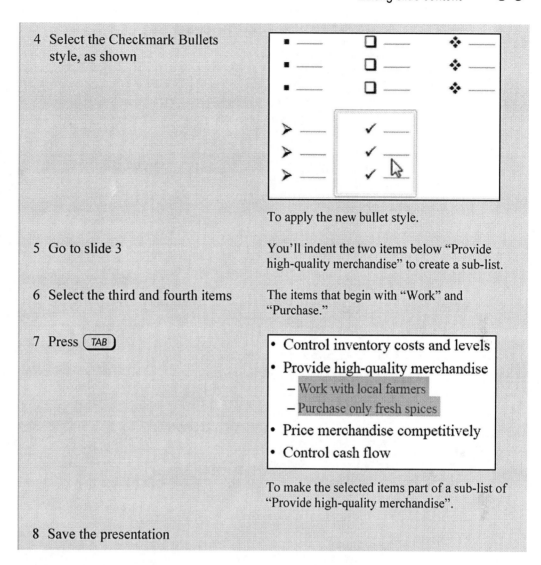

To apply the new bullet style.

5 Go to slide 3

You'll indent the two items below "Provide high-quality merchandise" to create a sub-list.

6 Select the third and fourth items

The items that begin with "Work" and "Purchase."

7 Press (TAB)

- Control inventory costs and levels
- Provide high-quality merchandise
  – Work with local farmers
  – Purchase only fresh spices
- Price merchandise competitively
- Control cash flow

To make the selected items part of a sub-list of "Provide high-quality merchandise".

8 Save the presentation

Numbered lists

Explanation

Similar to applying bullets to text, you can also apply automatic numbering to a list. When you create a numbered list (also called an ordered list), any item you add to the list is automatically numbered sequentially. To create a numbered list with the default numbering style, select the text and click the Numbering button.

To apply a specific numbering style:

1 Select the text.

2 In the Paragraph group, click the Numbering arrow to open the Numbering gallery.

3 Click a numbering style to apply it, and close the gallery.

A-5: Creating a numbered list

Here's how	Here's why
1 Go to the last slide	You'll modify the "Outstanding issues" slide.
2 Click anywhere in the bulleted text	To place the insertion point.
Press CTRL + A	To select all of the text in the placeholder.
3 In the Paragraph group, click as shown	To apply the default numbering style.
Observe the slide	The bulleted list is now a numbered list. You'll specify a different numbering style.
4 Click arrow next to the Numbering button, as shown	To open the Numbering gallery.
5 Click the indicated style	Next, you'll add another item to the list.
6 Place the insertion point at the end of the fifth line	Click after the word "program."
Press ↵ ENTER	To create a new line. The new item is numbered automatically. It appears transparent until you enter text.
7 Type **New employees**	To add another item to the list.
Press ↵ ENTER and type **Training**	To add a seventh item.
8 Save the presentation	

Paragraph formatting

Explanation

In addition to basic font styles, you can control the alignment, spacing, and indentation of paragraphs. *Paragraph formatting* is any formatting that applies to entire paragraphs, rather than individual characters or words. To apply any type of paragraph formatting, you can select any part of a paragraph, or you can simply place the insertion point in the paragraph.

Text alignment

When a paragraph is aligned left, the lines of text are set along the left side of the placeholder and the right side of the paragraph appears "ragged". The opposite is true for text aligned to the right. When you center text, each line is centered in its placeholder, which can create a ragged appearance on both sides but can be handy in many design contexts.

Another option is to use a justified alignment, in which the lines of text are aligned evenly on both sides of the placeholder. This can create some undesired spacing between words, however.

To align text, place the insertion point in a line of text or select multiple paragraphs. In the Paragraph group on the Home tab, click the Align Left, Center, Align Right, or Justify button. You can also use the alignment buttons on the Mini toolbar or set the alignment using the Paragraph dialog box.

Line spacing

To change line spacing (the amount of space between adjacent lines of text), place the insertion point in a line of text or select multiple paragraphs, click the Line Spacing button in the Paragraph group, and choose a line spacing value. Line spacing values are measured in lines (such as 1.5 lines).

You can also add space before or after a paragraph. Here's how:

1 Open the Paragraph dialog box by using either of these methods:
    - In the Paragraph group, click the Dialog Box Launcher.
    - Click the Line Spacing button and choose Line Spacing Options.
2 Under Spacing, enter a value in the Before or After box. (You can set line spacing in this dialog box, too.)
3 Click OK.

Indentation options

You can also use the Paragraph dialog box to set paragraph indentation and other styles. To indent the left side of all lines of a paragraph, enter a value in the Before text box. You can also set a first-line indent or a hanging indent value. If you don't want any indent, select "none" from the indent list. To apply the settings, click OK.

A-6: Controlling alignment and spacing

Here's how	Here's why
1 Go to slide 5	The slide titled "Performance."
2 Click the text in the top left paragraph	To place the insertion point.
3 In the Paragraph group, click ▤	(The Center button.) To align the paragraph to the center of text box.
Observe the second paragraph in the same text box	The second paragraph is not centered because it's a separate paragraph.
4 Drag to select both paragraphs in the left text box	
Click ▤	(The Align Right button is in the Paragraph group.) To align both paragraphs to the right. The text in the other text box is still aligned to the left, the default text alignment.
5 Select all of the text in the text box on the right	
Click ▤	(The Justify button.) To justify the selected text. Now the text is aligned on both sides of the text box. This alignment can lead to excessive spacing —for example the extra space around the word "productivity." This can affect readability in some contexts.
6 Verify that the right text box border is visible	
Hold down ⌷SHIFT⌷ and click in the left text box	To select both text boxes.
Click ▤ again	To justify the text in both text boxes.
7 Observe the current font size	In the Font group on the Home tab.
8 Click ▤▾	In the Paragraph group on the Home tab.
Choose **1.5**	To increase the line spacing in both text boxes.
9 Observe the current font size	The extra line spacing made the text overflow the boundaries of the right text box, so PowerPoint automatically adjusts the font size so that the text fits in the text boxes.

10	Go to slide 3	
11	Select the two sub-list items	You'll increase the left indent for the sub-list.
12	In the Paragraph group, click the Dialog Box Launcher	To open the Paragraph dialog box.
13	Under Indentation, in the Before text box, change the value to **1**	To specify a left indent of 1 inch.
	Click **OK**	To close the Paragraph dialog box.
14	Increase the spacing between the sub-list items to **1.5**	
15	Change the sub-list bullet items to arrows, as shown	

- Control inventory costs and levels
- Provide high-quality merchandise
  - ➢ Work with local farmers
  - ➢ Purchase only fresh spices
- Price merchandise competitively
- Control cash flow

16 Save and close the presentation

Topic B: Editing efficiently

This topic covers the following Microsoft Office Specialist exam objectives for PowerPoint 2013.

#	Objective
2.1	**Insert and Format Slides**
2.1.1	Add slide layouts

Explanation

You can move and copy text and objects from one slide to another or from one presentation to another. This can be a significant time saver as you reorganize the content in a presentation.

Replacing text

You can use the Find and Replace commands to quickly locate all instances of specific word or phrase in a presentation and replace those instances with new text. This can save you a lot of time because you don't have to scan through an entire presentation to find the text you're looking for, and you only have to type your replacement text once.

To find and replace text:

1 On the Home tab, in the Editing group, click Replace to open the Replace dialog box.

2 In the Find what box, type the text you want to find.

3 In the Replace with box, type the text you want to use.

4 Click Find Next to start the search. PowerPoint highlights the first instance of the text.

5 Click Replace to change that single occurrence, or click Replace All to change all occurrences of the text.

Do it!

B-1: Finding and replacing text

The files for this activity are in Student Data folder **Unit 3\Topic B**.

Here's how	Here's why
1 Open New project	From the current topic folder.
Save the presentation as **My New project**	In the current topic folder.
2 Verify that slide 1 is selected	
3 On the Home tab, in the Editing group, click [ab ac Replace]	(The Editing group is on the far right side of the window.) To open the Replace dialog box. The insertion point appears in the Find what box.
4 In the Find what box, type **merchandise**	You'll replace "merchandise" with "products."
5 In the Replace with box, type **products**	
6 Verify that "Match case" is cleared	To ensure that the search locates every instance of the word "merchandise," regardless of capitalization.
7 Click **Find Next**	The first instance of "merchandise" is highlighted in the presentation.
8 Click **Replace**	To change the selected word to "products." The next instance of "merchandise" is selected.
9 Click **Replace**	To replace the second instance of "merchandise" with "products." A message box appears, stating that the search is complete.
Click **OK**	To close the message box.
10 Close the Replace dialog box	
11 Save the presentation	

The Cut and Paste commands

Explanation

When you want to move text or an object from one location to another, you can use the Cut command. The Cut command removes the text or object from its original location so you can paste it elsewhere.

The Clipboard

When you cut or copy an item, it's placed temporarily on the Clipboard. The Windows Clipboard holds one item at a time and is cleared when you shut down your computer. However, you can overcome this limitation by using the Clipboard pane, which can hold up to 24 items.

After you cut or copy an item to the Clipboard, you can paste the item in a new location on the same slide, on another slide, or in a different presentation. To paste an item, you use the Paste command.

To move an item:

1   Select the item that you want to move.
2   In the Clipboard group, click the Cut button, or press Ctrl+X.
3   Place the insertion point where you want to insert the item.
4   In the Clipboard group, click the Paste button, or press Ctrl+V.

Pasting content as unformatted text

When you copy text from one slide to another, the text appears on the new slide with the formatting it displayed on the original slide. However, you can use the Paste Special command to paste an item using the formatting of its new slide. Here's how:

1   Place the insertion point where you want to paste the text.
2   In the Clipboard group, below the Clipboard icon, click Paste.
3   Click the Keep Text Only icon on the far right. (Or, you can click Paste Special to open the Paste Special dialog box, and select Unformatted Text.)

Drag and drop

You can also move text by using drag and drop. To drag text to a new location:

1   Select the text you want to move.
2   Press and hold the mouse button and drag the selected text to the new location.
3   Release the mouse button.

Do it!

B-2:   Cutting and dragging text

Here's how	Here's why
1 Go to slide 6	The last item in the list on this slide has not yet been accomplished, so you'll move it to the "Outstanding issues" slide.
2 Click before the word **Specifications**	To place the insertion point to the left of the word. You'll use the Shift+click method to select the text.
Point to the right of **initiative**	(Point to the right of the letter "e" at the end of the word.) To be sure not to select the bullet or any extra spaces.

	Press (SHIFT) and click	You'll move this bullet item into a numbered list on another slide, so it's important to select only the text.
3	In the Clipboard group, click [✂ Cut]	To remove the text from the slide and place it on the Clipboard.
4	Go to slide 7	
5	Click at the end of the last line	To place the insertion point.
	Press (↵ ENTER)	To add another item to the list.
6	Press (CTRL)+(V)	To paste the text from the Clipboard into the numbered list. The text is pasted with its original blue formatting. You'll undo this step and use Paste Special to paste the text without its original formatting.
7	Press (CTRL)+(Z)	To undo the last step.
8	Under the Clipboard icon, click **Paste**, as shown	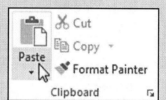

To open the Paste gallery. |
| | Click as shown |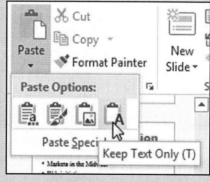

(The Keep Text Only button.) To paste the text and use the slide's current formatting. |
9	Triple-click **Building**	To select the text "Building a Website." You'll move this item above item 7.
10	Drag "Building a Website" just before the word "Training"	To move the item. The item numbering is updated automatically.
11	Save the presentation	

The Copy command

Explanation

When you want to copy an item from one location to another, you use the Copy command. As you'd expect, it places a copy of the selected item on the Clipboard, and the item you're copying remains in its original location.

To copy an item:

1 Select the item you want to copy.

2 In the Clipboard group, click the Copy button or press Ctrl+C.

3 Place the insertion point where you want to insert the item. This can be on the same slide, on another slide, or in another presentation.

4 Click the Paste button or press Ctrl+V.

The Paste Options button

The text you paste might be formatted differently than the text in the location where you want to paste it. You can choose whether the text should keep its formatting or inherit the formatting of the destination paragraph. To do so, click the Paste Options button, which appears to the right of any text you've pasted, and then choose an option from the drop-down menu.

Do it!

B-3: Copying text to another slide

Here's how	Here's why
1 At the end of the presentation, insert a new slide	Move to the last slide and click the New Slide button. Verify that the Title and Content slide layout is applied.
2 Go to slide 2	Scroll up.
Select **Outlander Spices**	Triple-click the text to select the entire line.
3 In the Clipboard group, click [📋 Copy]	To copy the title to the Clipboard. The copied text remains in its original location.
Go to the last slide	
4 Click the title placeholder	To place the insertion point.
Click [📋]	(The Clipboard icon.) To paste the text from the Clipboard into the title placeholder.
5 Observe the slide	The text is copied and the Paste Options button appears to the right of the text.

6	Press (CTRL)	(To open the Paste Options menu.) You can also click the Paste Options button.
	Click as shown	

To keep the formatting used in the source rather than the current slide.

7	Go to slide 5	
8	Copy the text in the left text box	(Click the left text box, press Ctrl+A, and then press Ctrl+C.) You'll paste the text in a new presentation.
9	Create a new blank presentation	On the File tab, click New, and then click Blank presentation.
10	Insert a new slide	Click the top portion of the New Slide button.
11	Click the content placeholder	(The large text box below the title placeholder.) To place the insertion point.
	Paste the text	Click the top portion of the Paste button, or press Ctrl+V.
12	Press (CTRL) + (A)	To select all the text in the text box.
13	Click	(In the Paragraph group.) To create bulleted text items.
14	Save the presentation as **Draft**	In the current topic folder.
	Close the presentation	To return to the other presentation.

The Clipboard pane

Explanation

In addition to the standard Windows Clipboard, you can also use the Clipboard pane. The Clipboard pane can store multiple items and is integrated across all Office programs. You can use it to copy multiple items in succession and then paste them, one at a time or simultaneously, into the preferred location(s) in a presentation. This procedure is called *collect and paste*. You can use it in any other Office program, including Word, Excel, Outlook, and Access.

To open the Clipboard pane, shown in Exhibit 3-2, click the Dialog Box Launcher in the bottom-right corner of the Clipboard group. The Clipboard pane appears to the left of the Slide pane.

Exhibit 3-2: The Clipboard pane

Collect and paste

You can collect items from any Office program with the Copy command and then paste them into other Office 2013 documents by using the Clipboard pane. For example, you can copy a chart in Excel, switch to Word and copy part of a document, and then switch to PowerPoint and paste both collected items, in any order.

To copy an item to the Office Clipboard, select the item and then click the Copy button or press Ctrl+C, just as you copy something to the standard Clipboard.

Using the Clipboard pane

The Clipboard pane can contain a maximum of 24 items. The contents of the Clipboard pane are not cleared when you close the pane. To clear the contents of the Clipboard pane, click the Clear All button. The following table describes the options on the Clipboard pane. You can also click Paste All to paste all collected items simultaneously at the insertion point. The items are pasted in the order in which they were collected.

Do it!

B-4: Using the Clipboard pane

Here's how	Here's why
1 At the end of the presentation, insert a new slide	Use the default Title and Content layout.
2 Type **Summary** as the title of the new slide	

3 In the Clipboard group, click the Dialog Box Launcher, as shown

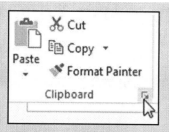

	To open the Clipboard pane. It contains the text that you pasted into the new presentation.
4 Click Clear All	(In the Clipboard pane.) To clear the Clipboard.
5 Go to slide 3	You'll copy items from this slide.
6 Copy the first two bullet items	(Drag to select the two items and then click the Copy button.) The Clipboard pane now contains the copied text, which appears as a single copied item.
7 Go to slide 6	
8 Copy the first two bullet items	The Clipboard pane now contains two items. The most recently copied text becomes the first item in the list.
9 Go to the last slide	The slide you just created.
10 Place the insertion point in the content placeholder	
11 In the Clipboard pane, point to the top item	(Do not click.) To display the item's arrow.
Click the arrow	A menu appears with two options. You choose Paste or Delete. You can also paste an item by clicking it.
Click the arrow again	To close the menu.
12 Click the top item	(In the Clipboard pane.) The slide now contains the items copied from slide 6.
13 Paste the second item from the Clipboard pane	Point to the second item in the Clipboard pane, click the arrow, and choose Paste.
Close the Clipboard pane	Click the X in the upper-right corner of the pane.
14 Save and close the presentation	

Unit summary: Editing slide content

Topic A   In this topic, you applied **basic text formatting**. You changed the **font, size,** and **color** of text, and you used the **Format Painter** to repeat text formatting. Then you modified **bullet styles** and created a **numbered list**. You also **formatted paragraphs** by controlling **alignment**, **line spacing**, and **indentation**.

Topic B   In this topic, you learned how to **replace text** and **move and copy text** to other slides. Finally, you learned how to use the **Clipboard pane** to copy and paste multiple items.

Review questions

1   What is the difference between character formatting and paragraph formatting?

2   What is the Mini toolbar?

3   True or false? You can display the Mini toolbar at any time by right-clicking the selected text.

4   What tool can you use to copy the formatting of selected text and apply it to other text?

5   What is the Clipboard?

6   How do you open the Replace dialog box?

7   How does the Clipboard pane differ from the Clipboard?

8   How do you open the Clipboard pane?

9   True or false? You can copy multiple copied items into a single location all at once.

Independent practice activity

In this activity, you'll replace text, apply basic formatting, and use the Format Painter to repeat that formatting.

The files for this activity are in Student Data folder **Unit 3\Unit summary**.

1 Open **Draft presentation**.

2 Save the file as **My Draft presentation**.

3 Find the text **Creating** and replace it with the word **Developing**.

4 Find the phrase **Markets in the East** and replace it with the phrase **Markets in the North**.

5 Apply bold formatting to the first slide's title, and increase the font size to 60.

6 On the second slide, give the title the font Trebuchet MS, make it bold, and apply a color of your choice. Align the title to the left.

7 Using the Format Painter, apply the title formatting on slide 2 to the titles of the other slides. (*Hint:* Double-click the Format Painter to keep it active for multiple applications.)

8 On the second slide, apply a new bullet style. Using the Format Painter, apply this change to the other bulleted lists in the presentation.

9 Save and close the presentation.

Unit 4

Working with shapes

Complete this unit, and you'll know how to:

A Create basic shapes and lines, and make basic shape modifications.

B Apply shape styles, apply fill and outline colors and effects, create a default shape, and move, rotate, resize, and align shapes.

C Add text content to shapes, format text in a shape, control text orientation, and create and format text boxes.

Topic A: Creating shapes

This topic covers the following Microsoft Office Specialist exam objectives for PowerPoint 2013.

#	Objective
1.0	**Create a Presentation**
1.1.1	Create blank presentations
2.2	**Insert and Format Shapes**
2.2.4	Insert shapes
2.2.5	Create custom shapes

Explanation

You can make your presentations appealing and engaging by applying shapes, such as rectangles, ovals, and arrows, to draw attention to content and enhance the overall look and feel of your slides.

Drawing tools

The tools you need to create shapes are on the Insert tab and the Drawing Tools | Format tab, which is context sensitive, meaning it's activated only when an action you take on a slide makes that set of tools relevant.

To create a shape:

1   In the Drawing group on the Home tab, scroll through the Shapes list, as shown in Exhibit 4-1, or click the More button at the bottom of the list's scrollbar. (You can also display the shapes gallery by clicking the Shapes button in the Illustrations group on the Insert tab.)

2   Select a tool, such as the Rectangle tool.

3   Point to the location where you want to begin drawing. The pointer changes to a crosshair.

4   Drag on the slide until the shape reaches the desired size. When you release the mouse button, the shape is automatically selected.

Another way to create a shape is to select a tool and click the slide. The specified shape is automatically drawn at a default size, which you can then modify.

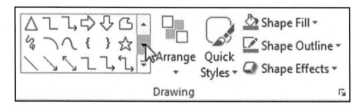

Exhibit 4-1: The Shapes list in the Drawing group on the Home tab

Exhibit 4-2 shows a selected rectangle and its sizing handles. You use the sizing handles to resize the shape. You can use the rotation handle at the top center of the shape to change its rotation angle.

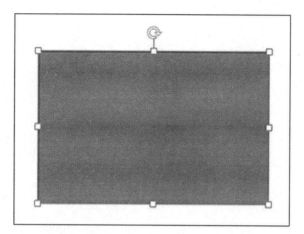

Exhibit 4-2: A selected rectangle showing its sizing handles and rotation handle

The Drawing Tools | Format tab

When you select a shape, the Drawing Tools | Format tab is added to the ribbon. This is a contextual tab that contains all the tools you need to create and format shapes. The Drawing Tools | Format tab automatically appears when you take a relevant action, such as creating or selecting a shape, inserting a picture, or drawing a diagram.

Do it!

A-1: Drawing basic shapes

Here's how	Here's why
1 Create a new blank presentation	On the File tab, click New. Then click Blank Presentation.
2 In the title placeholder, enter **Drawing Practice**	To give the presentation a name.
3 In the Slides group, click **New Slide**	To open the slide layout gallery.
Select **Blank**	To start with a blank slide.
4 Save the presentation as **My drawing practice**	In Student Data folder Unit 4\Topic A.
5 In the Drawing group, click as shown	(On the Home tab.) To select the Rectangle tool.
Point to the slide and observe the pointer	It appears as a crosshair to indicate that you can create a shape.

6	Drag to create a rectangle, as shown	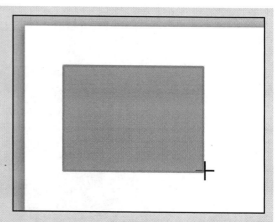
		The rectangle should be roughly one quarter the width of the slide.
	Release the mouse button	To complete the rectangle.
7	Observe the shape	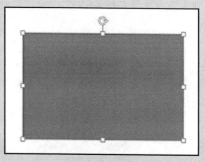
		The default fill color (blue) is automatically applied to the shape. Four corner sizing handles and four side sizing handles are displayed, plus a rotation handle at the top center of the shape.
	Observe the ribbon toolbar	The Drawing Tools | Format tab is automatically added to the ribbon when you create a shape. Contextual tabs appear only when you take an action that makes certain tools relevant.
8	Click a blank part of the slide	(To deselect the rectangle.) The Drawing Tools | Format tab no longer appears on the ribbon.
9	Select the rectangle	The Drawing Tools | Format tab appears again.
	Click the **Format** tab	To activate the tab. The drawing and shape tools are displayed.
10	In the Insert Shapes group, click as shown	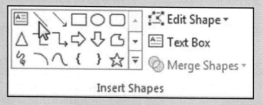
		To select the Line tool.

11 Press and hold ⟨SHIFT⟩	To constrain the line you'll draw to be vertical, horizontal, or at a 45-degree angle.
Point above and to the left of the rectangle and drag to the right	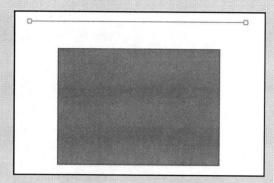
	Pressing Shift ensures that the line is drawn perfectly horizontally.
Press ⟨DELETE⟩	To delete the line.
12 Select the Arrow shape tool	In the Insert Shapes group.
Draw an arrow that points up to the rectangle	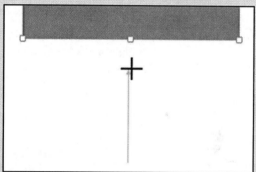
	Point below the rectangle, press and hold Shift, and drag up.
Deselect the arrow	Click a blank area of the slide or press Esc.
13 Delete the arrow	(Select it and press Delete.) You'll draw a block arrow.
14 Select the rectangle	To activate the Drawing Tools	Format tab.
Click as shown	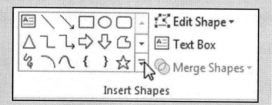
	To open the Shapes gallery.

15 Under Block Arrows, select the **Up Arrow** tool	
Starting below the rectangle, drag up and to the right	(Don't release the mouse button.) Dragging horizontally sets the shape's width, and dragging vertically sets its height.
Release the mouse button to complete the shape	
16 In the Insert Shapes group, click the Rounded Rectangle tool	
Click the slide	To insert a rounded rectangle at the default size. This is an alternative to dragging to create a shape. You can now resize the shape as needed.
17 Save your changes	

Changing shapes

Explanation

After you draw a shape, you can change it in several ways. For example, you can change a rectangle to an oval. To change a shape:

1 Select the shape you want to change.

2 Activate the Drawing Tools | Format tab if necessary.

3 In the Insert Shapes group, click the Edit Shape button and point to Change Shape to display the gallery.

4 Select the shape you want to use. The new shape replaces the old one, but retains any formatting that you had applied.

Modifying polygons

When you select a polygon, it might display one or more yellow *adjustment handles* in addition to the rotation handle and sizing handles. You can drag an adjustment handle to reshape the polygon. When you point to an adjustment handle, the pointer changes to a white arrowhead, as shown at the top of Exhibit 4-3.

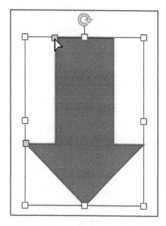

Exhibit 4-3: Pointing to an adjustment handle

Do it!   **A-2:   Modifying shapes**

Here's how	Here's why
1 Select the rectangle	You'll change the rectangle to an oval.
2 In the Insert Shapes group, click **Edit Shape**	(If necessary, activate the Drawing Tools | Format tab.) To display the Edit Shape menu.
3 Point to **Change Shape**	To display the gallery.
4 Under Basic Shapes, select **Oval**	To change the rectangle to an oval.
5 Select the arrow	(Click it.) You'll use its adjustment handles to modify the shape.
6 Point as shown	The yellow handles might be on the other side, depending on how you drew the shape.
Drag to the left, as shown	To change the size of the arrow stem.
7 Change the arrow to a shape of your choice	In the Insert Shapes group, click Edit Shape, point to Change Shape, and select a new shape.
8 Save and close the file	

Topic B: Formatting shapes

This topic covers the following Microsoft Office Specialist exam objectives for PowerPoint 2013.

#	Objective
2.2	**Insert and Format Shapes**
2.2.1	Modify shape backgrounds
2.2.2	Apply borders to shapes
2.2.3	Resize shapes
2.2.4	Insert shapes
2.2.5	Create custom shapes
2.2.6	Apply styles to shapes
2.3	**Order and Group Shapes and Slides**
2.3.3	Align and group shapes
2.3.4	Display gridlines

Explanation

One way to create a presentation that looks professional is to use a consistent color theme and apply styles thoughtfully. You can use the tools in the Shape Styles group on the Drawing Tools | Format tab to control a shape's fill color, outline color, and effects. You can also duplicate, move, resize, and rotate shapes to create the design elements you're looking for.

Shape styles

The Shape Styles group on the Drawing Tools | Format tab contains tools you can use to modify shape properties, including fill color, outline color, and effects. When you point to a style, the Live Preview feature shows how that style will look on the slide.

Shape fills

To change the fill color of a shape, select the shape. In the Shape Styles group on the Drawing Tools | Format tab, click Shape Fill to display a gallery and then select a color.

The following table describes the options in the Shape Fill gallery.

Option	Description
Theme Colors	Contains ten main color themes, each with five tints, for a total of 60 color swatches.
Standard Colors	Contains ten basic colors: Dark Red, Red, Orange, Yellow, Light Green, Green, Light Blue, Blue, Dark Blue, and Purple.
No Fill	Removes the fill color.
More Fill Colors	Opens the Colors dialog box, which contains two tabs: the Standard tab and the Custom tab. On the Custom tab, you can change the color model, tint, and transparency, and select from millions of colors.
Eyedropper	The Eyedropper allows you to match colors from within a presentation and also colors inside other applications, including Web browsers. This makes it easy to quickly apply the colors you want.
Picture	Opens the Insert Pictures screen, which you can use to add an image file as a shape fill. You can insert a picture from your computer, from Office.com, or directly from the Web via Bing search.
Gradient	Opens a gallery of gradients divided into two categories, Light Variations and Dark Variations.
Texture	Opens a gallery of textured fills, such as cloth, wood grain, and sand.

Shape outlines

To change an object's outline color, select the object. In the Shape Styles group, click the Shape Outlines arrow to display a gallery. Select a color, or choose one of the other options, such as No Outline, More Outline Colors, Weight, Dashes, or Arrows.

Shape effects

You can also apply effects to shapes, such as shadows, beveling, and 3-D effects. In the Shape Styles group, click the Shape Effects button to open a menu of effect categories. Then point to a category to open options in that category, and select the variation of you want to apply.

Creating a default shape format

When you have finished creating and formatting a shape, you can set your collection of formats as the new default. Here's how:

1   Verify that the desired shape is selected.
2   Right-click the selected shape and choose Set as Default Shape.

The next time you create a shape, it will automatically be formatted with the default fill, outline, and effects you've defined. However, it will not reproduce the size of the shape you used as the default, and the default settings apply only to the open presentation.

Do it!

B-1:   Applying shape styles

The files for this activity are in Student Data folder **Unit 4\Topic B**.

Here's how	Here's why
1 Open Shapes practice	From the current topic folder.
Save the presentation as **My Shapes practice**	
2 On slide 2, select the oval	
Click the **Format** tab	Under Drawing Tools on the ribbon.
3 In the Shape Styles group, point to the black background style	To see the Live Preview applied to the shape.
Click the first style	(The orange outline.) To apply the style to the shape.
4 In the Shape Styles group, click the More button, as shown	To open the styles gallery.
5 Click the **Colored Fill – Olive Green, Accent 3** style	(In the second row of styles.) Use the ScreenTips to identify the style.
6 Observe the oval	(Without deselecting it.) The fill color changes and an outline color is applied.
7 In the Shape Styles group, click **Shape Fill**	To display the Shape Fill options. You can apply theme colors, standard colors, and other styles.
Under Theme Colors, in the top row, click **Red, Accent 2**	The fill color changes.
8 Click **Shape Outline**	(In the Shape Styles group.) To display the Shape Outline options. You can set the shape to have no outline, change the line weight, apply dashes, and apply other outline styles.
Click the dark red color	(Under Theme Colors.) To make the shape outline dark red.

9 Click **Shape Effects**	To open the Shape Effects menu.
Point to each effect submenu	To view the galleries.
Point to **Preset**	To display the gallery of options. Currently, no 3-D effect is applied.
Under Presets, select **Preset 2**	(The second item in the first row.) Lighting and shading is applied to the shape to create the illusion of depth. This is an example of several styles you can apply to shapes.
10 Right-click the shape	To open a shortcut menu.
Select **Set as Default Shape**	The formats you have applied will be the new default settings when you create a shape in this presentation.
11 In the Insert Shapes group, select a new shape and click the slide	To create a new shape using the new default styles, but not the same size. This default formatting applies only to this presentation.
12 Delete the new shape	Select it and press Delete.
13 Save the presentation	

Duplicating shapes

Explanation

After you create a shape, you can duplicate it. Creating duplicates ensures that your shapes have a uniform size and format. For example, if you need to create several oval shapes, you can make one and then create duplicates of the original to ensure consistency. To duplicate a shape:

1. Select the shape.
2. On the Home tab, in the Clipboard group, click the arrow next to the Copy button and choose Duplicate. Or, press Ctrl+D to duplicate a shape.
3. Move the duplicated shape to the desired location.

You can also use the Copy and Paste commands, but using Ctrl+D is the fastest way to duplicate shapes.

Moving shapes

After you create or duplicate a shape, you'll probably want to move it. Here's how you can move a shape:

1. Point to the shape:
   - If the shape has a fill applied to it, point anywhere on the shape and the pointer shows a four-headed arrow.
   - If the shape has no fill, point to the edge of the shape but not to any of the sizing handles. The pointer shows to a four-headed arrow.
2. When the four-headed arrow appears, drag the shape to a new position.

Smart guides

When you're arranging shapes on a slide, you'll notice that one or more dotted lines will appear. These lines are called *smart guides*; they make it easy to align your shapes precisely. For example, if you have three ovals and you want the exact same spacing between them, smart guides appear as you drag the shapes to indicate precise alignment options, as shown in Exhibit 4-4. When a smart guide appears, release the mouse to complete the move.

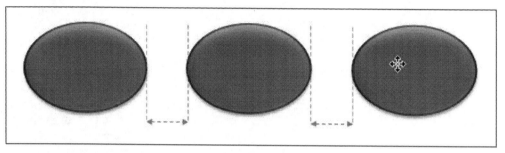

Exhibit 4-4: Smart guides help you to align your shapes precisely

Do it!

B-2:   Duplicating and moving objects

Here's how	Here's why
1 Select the oval	If necessary.
2 Copy the oval to the Clipboard	Click the Copy button on the Home tab, or press Ctrl+C.
3 Paste the oval	(Click the Paste button or press Ctrl+V.) The original shape is deselected. The pasted copy is offset to the right and down a bit.
Press (DELETE)	To delete the copied oval. No shapes are selected.
4 Select the oval	The Drawing Tools | Format tab is visible but not active.
Press (CTRL) + (D)	To duplicate the shape. You can also click the arrow next to the Copy button and choose Duplicate.
5 Point to the oval	The pointer shows a four-headed arrow, indicating you can move the shape in any direction.

Drag the oval to the right

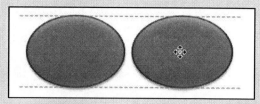

Smart guides appear to help you align the shapes precisely.

Release the mouse button

To complete the move.

6 With the oval selected, press ⌈ CTRL ⌉ + ⌈ D ⌉

To duplicate it again.

Move the third oval to the right an equal amount as the first two

The smart guides show equal spacing between the ovals, as shown in Exhibit 4-4.

7 Verify that the third oval is selected

8 On the Format tab, in the Shape Styles group, click as shown

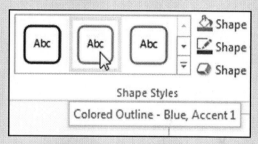

To change the outline and fill color.

9 Drag the selected oval to the left, as shown

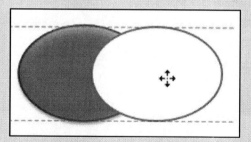

Drag so that it partially overlaps the oval next to it. The white fill covers the other oval where they overlap.

Release the mouse button

To place the shape.

10	Click **Shape Fill**	You will remove the white fill from the oval.
	Choose **No Fill**	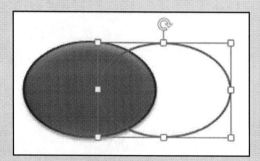

To remove the fill from the object. It's now a transparent oval, so the shape underneath it shows through.

11	Point inside the transparent oval	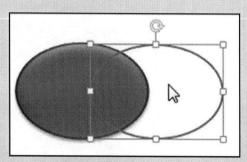

The pointer does not show the four-headed arrow because there is no longer a fill applied to this shape—you can't move it by dragging from its center. You need to drag from the outline.

12	Point to the oval's outline	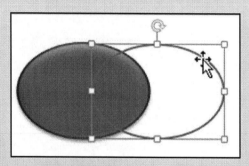

The pointer shows the four-headed arrow to indicate that you can move the object.

13	Drag to the oval to the right so that all three are equally spaced	s
14	Save the presentation	

Resizing shapes

Explanation

After you create a shape, you can change its size as needed. To resize a shape:

1   Select the object. The rotation handle and sizing handles appear.

2   Do one of the following:

  • Point to a corner sizing handle if you want adjust the shape's width and height at the same time. The pointer changes to a diagonal double-headed arrow.

  • Point to a side sizing handle if you want to increase or decrease the shape's width. The pointer changes to a horizontal double-headed arrow.

  • Point to the top or bottom sizing handle if you want to adjust the shape's height. The pointer changes to a vertical double-headed arrow.

3   Drag the sizing handle until the shape reaches the desired size, and then release the mouse button.

If you want to resize a shape to specific dimensions, you can enter numeric values in the Shape Height and Shape Width boxes in the Size group on the Drawing Tools | Format tab. If you want to maintain the shape's proportions as you resize it, hold down the Shift key as you drag to resize the shape.

Do it!

B-3:   Resizing a shape

Here's how	Here's why
1 Click the **Home** tab	If necessary.
2 Click **New Slide**	To display the slide gallery.
Select **Title Only**	To add a new slide with the Title Only layout.
3 In the title placeholder, type **Monthly Sales Awards**	You'll create star shapes to contain the names of sales employees.
4 In the Drawing group, open the Shapes gallery	(Click the More button to open the Shapes gallery.) You'll create a star shape.
5 Under Stars and Banners, select the **16-Point Star**	You'll use this tool to create a star.
6 Click below the title placeholder	To create a star using the default size. Again, the shape uses the default styles you set.
7 Point to the bottom-right corner sizing handle, as shown	The pointer changes to a diagonal two-way arrow, indicating that you can drag in either direction to set the width and height.

8	Drag down and to the right about an inch	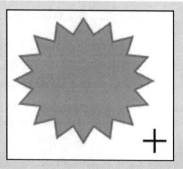
		To change the shape's height and width.
	Release the mouse button	To finish resizing.
9	Point to the bottom-center sizing handle	The pointer changes to a vertical two-way arrow, indicating that you can change the shape's height.
	Drag up about half an inch	(Release the mouse button when done.) To reduce the height of the star by about half an inch.
10	Point to the center-right sizing handle	The pointer changes to a horizontal two-way arrow, indicating that you can change the shape's width.
	Drag to the left about half an inch	To reduce the width of the star by about half an inch.
11	Activate the Drawing Tools | Format tab	You'll set precise height and width values.
12	In the Size group, click in the Shape Height box, as shown	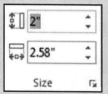
		To select the current value.
	Type **2.5** and press (↵ ENTER)	To set the height to 2.5 inches.
13	Select the value in the Shape Width box	
	Type **2.5** and press (↵ ENTER)	To set the width to 2.5 inches.
14	Save the presentation	

Rotating shapes

Explanation   You can change the rotation angle of a shape. Here's how:

1 Select the shape. The rotation handle and sizing handles appear.
2 Point to the rotation handle. The pointer changes to a black circle with an arrow, indicating a rotating motion.
3 Drag in a clockwise or counter-clockwise motion and release the mouse button when you reach the desired result.

If you want to rotate an object to a specific angle, select it and then, in the Size group on the Drawing Tools | Format tab, click the Dialog Box Launcher to open the Format Shape pane. In the Rotation box, enter the desired angle value and close the pane.

Do it!   ### B-4:   Rotating a shape

Here's how	Here's why
1 Go to slide 2	You'll rotate a shape.
Select the middle oval	
Click the rotation handle, as shown	
	The pointer changes to a black circle with an arrow, indicating a rotating motion.
Drag down and to the right, as shown	
	To rotate the oval clockwise.
2 In the Size group, click the Dialog Box Launcher	(On the Drawing Tools | Format tab.) To open the Format Shape pane on the right side of the window.
Observe the Rotation box	It shows the shape's current angle of rotation.
In the Rotation box, enter **90**	To rotate the oval 90 degrees.
Close the Format Shape pane	
3 Save the presentation	

Aligning shapes

Explanation

You can use the Align menu to arrange shapes on a slide. Here's how:

1 Select one or more shapes to align.
2 Click the Drawing Tools | Format tab.
3 In the Arrange group, click the Align button and select an option.

How shapes are aligned using the commands in the Align menu will depend on whether the Align to Slide option is checked. If it is, all alignments are relative to the slide. If it's not selected, alignments are calculated relative to other shapes. The following table describes the options in the Align menu.

Option	Description
Align Left	Aligns the selected shapes to the left side of the slide.
Align Center	Aligns the selected shapes to the center of the slide, but does not affect the vertical position.
Align Right	Aligns the selected shapes to the right side of the slide.
Align Top	Aligns the selected shapes to the top of the slide.
Align Middle	Aligns the selected shapes to the middle of the slide.
Align Bottom	Aligns the selected shapes to the bottom of the slide.
Distribute Horizontally	Evenly distributes the horizontal space between the selected shapes.
Distribute Vertically	Evenly distributes the vertical space between the selected objects.
Align to Slide	When this option is checked, the Align commands align objects with the slide, rather than with one another.
Align selected objects	When this option is checked, the Align commands align objects with one another, rather than with the slide.

If the Align to Slide option is not selected in the Align menu, left alignments will be relative to the leftmost shape, right alignments to the rightmost shape, and so on.

Gridlines

You can use gridlines to help you to arrange items precisely. *Gridlines* are intersecting dotted lines that appear on a slide. They are not part of the slide content. To activate gridlines, click the View tab and select Gridlines in the Show group.

Do it!   **B-5:   Aligning shapes**

Here's how	Here's why
1 Go to slide 3	
2 Select the star	
Duplicate the shape twice	Press Ctrl+D twice to create two copies.
3 Arrange the stars as shown	
4 Hold down [CTRL] and select the other two stars	So that all three stars are selected.
Release [CTRL]	
5 On the Format tab, click **Align**	(In the Arrange group.) To display the Align menu.
Select **Align to Slide**	(If necessary.) By default, alignments are set to other shapes.
From the Align menu, choose **Align Middle**	To arrange the stars in a line in the middle of the slide.
6 Click **Align** and choose **Distribute Horizontally**	To evenly distribute the horizontal space between the stars.
7 Click the **View** tab	
In the Show group, select **Gridlines**	Dotted gridlines appear on the slide. This is not part of the slide content; the gridlines are designed to help you to arrange content.
8 Verify that all three shapes are selected	
Press [↑] nine times	To move the three stars up simultaneously so that they are aligned to the dotted gridline, closer to the slide title.
9 Clear **Gridlines**	(In the Show group.) To hide the gridlines.
10 Save and close the presentation	

The image referenced shows a slide titled "Monthly Sales Awards" with three star shapes arranged on it.

Topic C: Applying content to shapes

This topic covers the following Microsoft Office Specialist exam objectives for PowerPoint 2013.

#	Objective
2.2	**Insert and Format Shapes**
2.2.5	Create custom shapes
2.2.6	Apply styles to shapes
3.1	**Insert and Format Text**
3.1.2	Create multiple columns in a single shape

Explanation

Shapes by themselves can enhance the overall message you want to convey in a presentation, but in many cases, your text content is what makes your message effective.

Inserting text in a shape

When you add text to a shape, the text becomes part of the object and moves along with it on a slide. However, if you resize the shape, the text is not automatically resized along with it.

To add text to a shape, select the shape and begin typing. By default, the text is centered in the object and the color will conform to theme style that is applied, if any. You can change the alignment, colors, and other styles of the text after you type.

Do it!

C-1: Adding text to shapes

The files for this activity are in Student Data folder **Unit 4\Topic C**.

Here's how	Here's why
1 Open Monthly sales awards	From the current topic folder.
Save the presentation as **My Monthly sales awards**	
2 On slide 2, select the center star	
3 Type **Morgan Smith**	To add the text within the shape. The text is automatically formatted to conform to the shape's current design theme. The text is also automatically centered in the star.
4 Select the left star	
5 Type **Peyton Miller**	
6 Select the right star and type **Sean Green**	
7 Save the presentation	

Formatting text in shapes

Explanation

You can format text in shapes the same way would format any other text. Select the text or the shape containing the text, and use the options on the Mini toolbar or in the Font group on the Home tab. You can change the font, size, and color of the text, and make it bold, italic, underlined, or shadowed. You can also change text styles by changing its shape's design theme.

Do it!

C-2: Formatting text in a shape

Here's how	Here's why
1 Point to Peyton Miller	The pointer changes to an I-beam, which is standard for text editing.
Click once	To place the insertion point in the text.
Press CTRL + A	To select all of the text in the shape. You could also drag to select the text.
2 Observe the selection	There's a white outline around the text, indicating that it's selected.
3 On the Home tab, from the Font list, select **Arial Black**	To change the font face to an option that's bolder and slightly larger.
4 Double-click **Format Painter**	(In the Clipboard group on the Home tab.) To copy the text formatting to the other stars.
Click the text **Morgan**	To apply the text formatting to this text.
Click the text **Smith**	To apply the text formatting.
5 Apply the formatting to the text **Sean Green**	
6 Click **Format Painter**	To de-activate the Format Painter.
7 Save the presentation	

Drawing text boxes

Explanation

By default, when you select a shape and type text, PowerPoint automatically creates a text box. You can also draw a text box on a slide and then enter text in it. As you add text to a text box, its width remains constant but the height adjusts to fit the text.

To create a text box and add text:

1 Click the Text Box button in any of the following ribbon groups:
  - The Drawing group on the Home tab
  - The Text group on the Insert tab
  - The Insert Shapes group on the Drawing Tools | Format tab

2 Drag to create a text box and begin typing, or click the slide and begin typing.

3 Resize, format, and move the text box as needed.

To resize a text box, click it so that selection handles appear along the edges and on the corners; then drag a selection handle. To delete a text box, select it and press Delete.

Text formatting and orientation

You can format the text in a text box by using the same techniques you use to format other slide text. You can also set the orientation for the text in a text box. For example, you can rotate the text 90 degrees or 270 degrees within a text box. To change the orientation of text in a text box:

1 Click the Home tab.

2 In the Paragraph group, click the Text Direction button and choose a text direction.

3 Resize and move the text box as necessary to create the desired result.

Do it!

C-3: Creating text boxes

Here's how	Here's why
1 Create a new blank slide	(On the Home tab, click New Slide and then click Blank.) You'll add text listing new kiosk locations.
2 Click the **Insert** tab	
3 In the Text group, click **Text Box**	You'll create a text box displaying vertical text for the slide's title.
4 Drag to draw the text box as shown	

5 Type **New kiosk locations**

As you type, the text box changes size to optimally fit the current text size.

Select the text

Press Ctrl+A.

Set the font to **Arial Black**, with a font size of **40**

Again the text box automatically sizes to accommodate the text.

6 In the Paragraph group, click **Text Direction**

To display the Text Direction menu.

Choose **Rotate all text 270°**

The text is rotated but looks jumbled in the text box. You'll resize the text box.

7 Point to the bottom-right handle on the text box, as shown

The pointer changes to a two-headed arrow.

Drag down and to the left until it fits on one vertical line, as shown

(Drag to the bottom-left corner of the slide.) To create a text box with vertical text.

8 On the Format tab, click **Align** and choose **Align Middle**

To align the text box in the middle of the slide, without centering it on the slide.

Click Align and choose Align Left

To align the text box to the left edge of the slide.

Formatting text boxes

In addition to formatting text in a text box, you can format the text box itself. You can apply a fill, border, and effects. Here's how:

1 Select the text box.

2 Click the Drawing Tools | Format tab.

3 Apply formatting by using options in the Shape Styles group:

- Click Shape Fill and choose a fill color.
- Click Shape Outline and choose an outline color, weight, and style.
- Click Shape Effects and choose an effect.

Text alignment and margins

With the tools in the Paragraph group on the Home tab, you can change the alignment of text within a text box and change the internal margins for a text box. Here's how:

- Click a horizontal alignment button (Left, Center, Right, Justify).
- Click the Align Text button and choose Top, Middle, or Bottom to specify vertical alignment within the text box.
- Click the Align Text button and choose More Options to open the Format Shape pane with Text Options active, and set alignment and margin options.

Creating columns

You can format a text box to display its text in columns. To do so, select the text box. Then, in the Paragraph group on the Home tab, click the Columns button and choose the number of columns you want. The effect might not be immediately apparent; you might need to resize the text box to achieve the desired result.

You can also click the Columns button and choose More Columns to open the Columns dialog box. Specify the number of columns and a spacing value between columns, and then click OK.

Creating a custom default text box format

After you have formatted a text box, you can define its settings as the new default formatting for text boxes. Here's how:

1 Verify that the formatted text box is selected. If the text box has no fill, you'll need to select the edge.

2 Right-click the selected text box and choose Set as Default Text Box.

Changing the shape of a text box

You can change the shape of a text box to another shape. Here's how:

1 Select the text box you want to change.

2 On the Drawing Tools | Format tab, in the Insert Shapes group, click the Edit Shape button and point to Change Shape to display a gallery of shapes.

3 Select the shape you want to use. The new shape replaces the old one, but any formatting you had applied to the old shape is retained.

Do it!

C-4: Formatting text boxes

Here's how	Here's why
1 On the Format tab, in the Shape Styles group, click **Shape Fill**	
Select a light blue color	To apply the fill color to the text box.
2 Click **Shape Outline** and select a dark blue color	To apply the outline color to the text box.
3 Click **Shape Outline** and point to **Weight**	To open the outline weight options.
Select **3 pt**	To increase the outline weight (thickness).
4 Click **Shape Effects** and point to **Bevel**	To open the bevel options.
Click the Cool Slant bevel effect, as shown	To apply a bevel effect.
5 Click the **Home** tab	You'll change the text box's margin settings.
6 In the Paragraph group, click **Align Text**	
Choose **More Options...**	To open the Format Shape pane on the right side of the window. The Text Options are displayed.
7 Change the Left margin value to **0.2**	
Change the Right margin value to **0.2**	To increase the left and right margins in the text box, thereby increasing the box's width.
8 Verify that the Top and Bottom margin values are set to **0.05**	
Close the Format Shape pane	
9 Click the **Format** tab	
In the Size group, enter **7.2** in the Shape Height box	To change the height of the text box.

10	Set the text box width to **1**	
11	Click **Align**	In the Arrange group.
	Select **Align Middle**	To align the text box vertically to the middle of the slide.
12	Create another text box as shown	

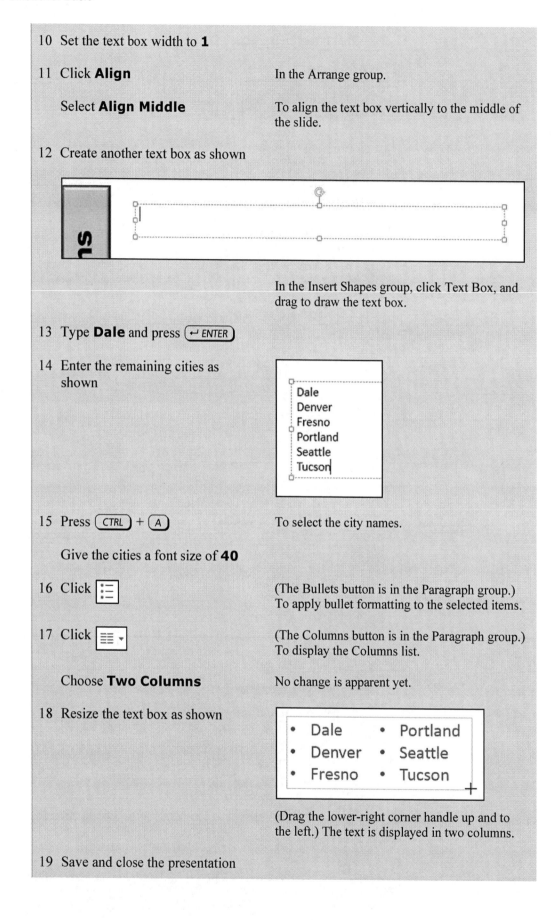

		In the Insert Shapes group, click Text Box, and drag to draw the text box.
13	Type **Dale** and press ⏎ ENTER	
14	Enter the remaining cities as shown	Dale Denver Fresno Portland Seattle Tucson
15	Press CTRL + A	To select the city names.
	Give the cities a font size of **40**	
16	Click ▤	(The Bullets button is in the Paragraph group.) To apply bullet formatting to the selected items.
17	Click ▤ ▾	(The Columns button is in the Paragraph group.) To display the Columns list.
	Choose **Two Columns**	No change is apparent yet.
18	Resize the text box as shown	• Dale • Portland • Denver • Seattle • Fresno • Tucson
		(Drag the lower-right corner handle up and to the left.) The text is displayed in two columns.
19	Save and close the presentation	

Unit summary: Working with shapes

Topic A   In this topic, you learned how to create and modify basic **shapes** and **lines**, and you learned how to **change a shape** to another shape.

Topic B   In this topic, you learned how to apply **shape styles**. You learned how to apply **fill color** and **outline color**, **effects**, and create a **custom default shape**. You also learned how to **duplicate** and **move shapes**, **resize** and **rotate shapes**, and **align shapes**.

Topic C   In this topic, you learned how to apply **text content** to shapes, **format text** in a shape, control text **orientation**, and create and format **text boxes**.

Independent practice activity

In this activity, you'll create the shapes and content shown in Exhibit 4-5.

1 Create a new blank presentation. Insert a new blank slide.

2 On the Home tab, in the Drawing group, display the Shapes gallery and click the Horizontal Scroll shape (under Stars and Banners).

3 Drag to draw the shape across the slide.

4 Apply a shape style of your choice. Apply a fill color, an outline color, and effects of your choice. (*Hint:* Use the Drawing Tools | Format tab.)

5 Add the text **Employee of the Month** to the shape. Apply the formatting of your choice to the text. Resize the banner object to display all of the text on one line, if necessary.

6 Draw a text box at the bottom of the slide, type the text **Award**, and apply formatting of your choice.

7 Use the rotation handle to rotate the banner object slightly.

8 Align the banner with the center of the slide.

9 Move the Award text box near the banner. Compare your slide to Exhibit 4-5 and make modifications as necessary.

10 Save the presentation as **Employee of the Month** in the current unit summary folder.

11 Close the presentation.

Exhibit 4-5: Employee of the Month banner shape and Award text box.

Review questions

1 After you create a shape, how can you change its shape type?

2 To change fill colors and outline colors and apply effects to a selected shape, you use the commands in which group?

A Insert Shapes

B Shape Styles

C Design

D Formatting

3 List two methods you can use to duplicate a shape without using Copy and Paste.

4 True or false? By default, when you change the size of text in a text box, the text box size changes to accommodate the text size.

5 How do you make a formatted shape the new default shape in a presentation?

6 True or false? When you activate gridlines, they will appear in the finished product.

7 How do you add text to a shape?

8 What are smart guides?

A Gridlines that appear as a backdrop on the slide.

B Dotted lines that appear as you drag shapes near other shapes; they make it easy to align your shapes precisely.

C Lines that you draw on a slide.

D Dotted lines that appear as you drag shapes near other shapes; they are actual content that is part of the finished product.

U n i t   5

Graphics

Complete this unit, and you'll know how to:

A Create and modify text effects by using WordArt, and apply WordArt styles to normal text.

B Insert and modify images, arrange and group items, and control the stacking order of overlapping elements.

Topic A: WordArt

This topic covers the following Microsoft Office Specialist exam objectives for PowerPoint 2013.

#	Objective
1.1	**Create a Presentation**
1.1.1	Create blank presentations
3.1	**Insert and Format Text**
3.1.1	Change text to WordArt
3.1.4	Apply formatting and styles to text

Explanation

You can use WordArt to apply special formatting to text. *WordArt* is a text object with predefined effects that you can customize. Exhibit 5-1 shows an example of WordArt.

Exhibit 5-1: An example of WordArt

Inserting and editing WordArt

To insert a WordArt object:

1 Click the Insert tab.
2 In the Text group, click WordArt to open the WordArt gallery.
3 Select a WordArt style to add a WordArt object in the center of the slide. The text is selected and ready for you to type.
4 Type to enter text in the WordArt object.

You can edit WordArt text just as you edit any other text. Click to place the insertion point in the WordArt object, or select one or more words, and begin editing.

Resizing and rotating WordArt

You can resize and rotate WordArt just as you would a graphic or shape. Select the object to display the rotation handle and sizing handles, and then do any of the following:

- Drag a corner sizing handle to change the object's height and width, causing the text to re-flow within the object.
- Drag a sizing handle on the left or right side of the object to change only the width.
- Drag a sizing handle on the top or bottom of the object to change only the height.
- Drag the rotation handle to change its rotation angle.

Do it!   **A-1:   Inserting and modifying WordArt**

Here's how	Here's why
1 Create a new, blank presentation	
Save the presentation as **New Web site**	In Student Data folder Unit 5\Topic A.
2 In the title placeholder, type **Outlander Spices**	
In the subtitle placeholder, type **New Web Site Launch**	You'll create a presentation that introduces a new Web site.
3 Insert a new slide using the Title Only layout	
4 In the title placeholder, type **Web Site Redesign**	To give the slide a title.
5 Click the **Insert** tab	
6 In the Text group, click **WordArt**	To display the WordArt gallery.
Observe the WordArt gallery	It contains a variety of WordArt styles.
7 Select the **Fill – White, Outline – Accent 1** style	(In the top row, fourth from the left.) To insert a WordArt object in the center of the slide.
Observe the WordArt object	
	The placeholder text is selected and pre-formatted. When you begin typing, the text is replaced.
8 Type **Launches Next Week!**	To replace the placeholder text.
9 Point to the WordArt border	
	(Don't point to a handle.) The pointer shows a four-headed arrow, indicating you can move the object.
Drag to the left so that it's aligned with the slide title	As you drag, a smart guide will appear to show you the alignment with the title.

10 From the rotation handle, drag counter-clockwise, as shown

To rotate the object at a slight angle.

11 Save the presentation

Formatting WordArt

Explanation

After you've created a WordArt object, you can edit it, change the WordArt style, and customize it with additional formatting.

Selecting WordArt text

Before you apply a new WordArt style, make sure you have selected the text correctly. If you click to place the insertion point in the WordArt text and then apply a style, it will apply only to the word that contains the insertion point. You can drag to select the WordArt text you want to format, or you can select all the text in a WordArt object by selecting the WordArt object itself (by clicking one of its edges) or by clicking the WordArt text and pressing Ctrl+A to select it all.

Commands in the WordArt Styles group

When a WordArt object is selected, the Drawing Tools | Format tab appears. On this tab, the WordArt Styles group includes the Text Fill, Text Outline, and Text Effects buttons, which are described in the following table. You can also select a preset style from the WordArt Styles gallery.

Button	Description
Text Fill	Contains options to set the fill color of the text, remove a fill, or add a gradient or a texture.
Text Outline	Contains options to set the outline color of the text.
Text Effects	Opens a gallery of preset styles that you can apply, such as Shadow, Reflection, Glow, Bevel, 3-D Rotation, and Transform.

Creating WordArt from normal text

You can also apply WordArt styles to normal text. To do so, simply select the text and choose a style from the WordArt Styles gallery. You can then further modify the formatting as needed.

Do it!   **A-2:   Applying WordArt styles**

Here's how	Here's why
1 Click the word **Next**	(To place the insertion point in the word.) You'll change the formatting.
On the Format tab, expand the WordArt Styles gallery	(Click the More button below the scrollbar on the WordArt styles gallery.) To view more WordArt styles.
2 Click the orange style in the top row	(To apply the style to the word "Next".) To apply the formatting to all of the text, you can select it all by dragging or pressing Ctrl+A, or by selecting the text box.
3 Select the WordArt object	(Click any one of its dotted borders to select it.) You could also drag to select the text.
Apply the same style	To format all of the text the same.
4 Click **Text Fill**	(In the WordArt Styles group.) To open the Text Fill menu.
From the Theme Colors list, select a light blue color	
5 Click **Text Outline**	(In the WordArt Styles group.) To open the Text Outline menu.
From the Theme Colors list, select the dark blue color	
6 Click **Text Effects**	(In the WordArt Styles group.) To open the Text Effects menu.
Point to **Shadow**	To open the text shadow options.
Under Outer, select the first shadow style	To apply a drop shadow effect.
7 Press ⦅ESC⦆	To deselect the text box.
8 Triple-click **Web Site Redesign**	
9 Apply a WordArt style of your choice	To apply a WordArt style to normal text.
10 Deselect the text	
11 Save and close the presentation	

Topic B: Pictures

This topic covers the following Microsoft Office Specialist exam objectives for PowerPoint 2013.

#	Objective
2.3	**Order and Group Shapes and Slides**
2.3.3	Align and group shapes
3.5	**Insert and Format Images**
3.5.1	Resize images
3.5.2	Crop images
3.5.3	Apply effects
3.5.4	Apply styles

Explanation

You can use images to convey ideas and information that can be difficult to express in words. With that in mind, it's a good idea to add images to a presentation whenever they are useful. After you insert an image on a slide, you can modify it in several ways.

Inserting pictures

There are many ways to insert pictures in your presentation slides. Here's one way:

1   Click the Insert tab.
2   In the Images group, click Pictures. The Insert Picture dialog box opens.
3   Navigate to the image file you want to use, select it, and click Insert. (You can also double-click the file in the dialog box.)

You can also use a slide layout to insert a picture. Here's how:

1   Insert a new slide using the Title and Content, Two Content, Comparison, Content with Caption, or Picture with Caption layout.
2   On the slide, click the Pictures icon to open the Insert Picture dialog box.
3   Locate and select the desired file, and click Insert (or double-click the file in the dialog box).

After you insert a picture, it is selected automatically, and the Picture Tools | Format tab is activated so that you can modify the image as needed.

Inserting images obtained online

PowerPoint 2013 makes it easier than ever to locate and insert the images you want to use in your presentations. On the Insert tab, you can now click the Online Pictures button to open the Insert Pictures screen, shown in Exhibit 5-2. You can search the Office.com Clip Art collection, or you can search for images using the Bing search engine and insert images into your presentation directly.

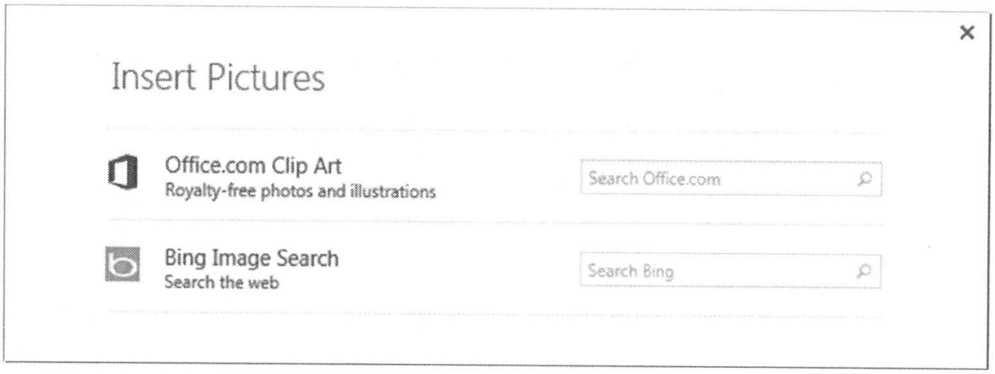

Exhibit 5-2: The new Insert Pictures screen

The images you find in the Office.com Clip Art collection are free to use; they include both photographs and illustrations. If you want to insert an image using the Bing Image Search feature, by default the images you'll see are licensed under Creative Commons so they're free to use. To view images using a standard Web search, you can click the Show all web results button. However, before you insert any image, it's important that you understand what the licensing terms are for that image.

Do it!

B-1: Inserting pictures

The files for this activity are in Student Data folder **Unit 5\Topic B**.

Here's how	Here's why
1 Open New Web site	From the current topic folder.
Save the presentation as **My New Web site**	
2 On the Insert tab, in the Images group, click **Pictures**	To open the Insert Picture dialog box.
Insert the **Spice bottle** image	In the current topic folder, click Spice bottle, and click Insert.
3 Observe the ribbon toolbar	The Picture Tools | Format tab is active. This is a contextual tab that appears when you select an image file.
4 Use the (←) and (↓) keys to move the image as shown	
	 If your keyboard does not have arrow keys, drag from an edge to move the image.

5	Go to slide 2	
6	On the Insert tab, click **Pictures**	To open the Insert Picture dialog box.
	Insert the **Web site** image	The slide title is visible, but the "Launch Next Month!" WordArt object is hidden beneath the picture.
7	Save the presentation	You'll continue working on this presentation.
8	Click **Online Pictures**	(On the Insert tab.) To open the Insert Pictures screen, shown in Exhibit 5-2.
	Observe the screen	From this screen you can search the Office.com ClipArt collection or search for images using the Bing search engine, and insert images into your presentation directly.
9	In the Bing Image Search box, type **cinnamon sticks**	
	Press ⏎ ENTER	Several images that match the search keywords are displayed in the Insert Pictures screen. You can select an image and click Insert.
	Read the message with the yellow background	The images that appear in the Insert Pictures screen are filtered by default so that you can view pictures that are licensed under Creative Commons.
10	Close the Insert Pictures screen	Click the X in the upper-right corner of the screen to close it.

Working with pictures

Explanation
There are many ways you can apply and customize your pictures in PowerPoint 2013. When you work with images, the Picture Tools | Format tab is displayed which provides several tools and options divided into distinct groups on the ribbon toolbar.

Image editing tools in the Adjust group

The Adjust group on the Picture Tools | Format tab, shown in Exhibit 5-1, contains the tools you'll use most frequently to edit selected images. For example, you can apply image corrections, modify the color balance, and apply artistic effects.

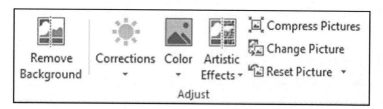

Exhibit 5-3: The Adjust group on the Picture Tools | Format tab

Corrections

You can change an image's brightness, contrast, or sharpness. First, select the image and click Corrections to display the style gallery. Before you click to apply a setting, you can point to a Sharpen/Soften option or a Brightness/Contrast option to see how each setting will affect the image.

You're not limited to the preset options; you can apply custom corrections. Open the Corrections gallery and choose Picture Corrections Options to open the Format Picture task pane. As you change settings, you can see them applied to the selected image.

Color

You can make color adjustments to tie in an image with a slide's color scheme. Select the image and click the Color button on the Format tab. In the gallery, select a preset from the Color Saturation, Color Tone, or Recolor groups. You can apply one preset from each of the three categories.

To apply custom colorization, select the picture, open the Color gallery, and select Picture Color Options to open the Format Picture task pane, which contains several options and controls that you can use to customize your picture.

Artistic Effects

The Artistic Effects tool contains several preset effects you can use to alter an image. Select the picture and click Artistic Effects to open the gallery. Point to an option to preview its effect on the image, and click an option to apply it.

Compress Pictures

Images are often an important component of a presentation, but each image adds to the overall file size of the presentation. To reduce the file size of your presentations without compromising image quality, you can use the Compress Pictures tool. Select the picture(s) you want to compress and click the Compress Pictures button to open the Compress Pictures dialog box. Specify compression and output settings, and click OK.

Change Picture

Let's say you've taken the time to resize an image and apply other formats and effects to it, but you determine that you need to replace it with another picture. You can use the Change Picture tool to quickly replace the image while maintaining all the formatting you had applied to the previous image. Select the image and click the Change Picture button. This opens the Insert Pictures screen. You can insert an image from your computer, from Office.com, or from a Bing image search.

Re-sizing an image

To re-size an image, you can drag from any of its resize handles. Drag from a corner resize handle to resize the image proportionally. You can also select the image and set the height and width manually by entering values in the Height and Width boxes in the Size group on the Picture Tools | Format tab.

Reset Picture

To remove the formatting applied to an image, select the picture and click the Reset Picture button. The image returns to its original state.

Tools in the Picture Styles, Arrange, and Size groups

The following table describes some of the tools in the Picture Styles, Arrange, and Size groups on the Picture Tools | Format tab.

Button	Description
Picture Border	Opens the Picture Border gallery. You can set border style, color, and weight (thickness) or remove an existing border.
Picture Effects	Opens the Picture Effects gallery. You can apply effects such as shadow, reflection, glow, soft edges, bevel, and 3-D rotation.
Bring Forward	Brings the selected object forward one position in the stacking order when items on a slide overlap. You can also click the arrow and choose Bring to Front to bring the selected object in front of all other objects on the slide.
Send Backward	Sends the selected object back one position in the stacking order. Click the arrow and choose Send to Back to send the selected object behind all other objects on the slide.
Selection Pane	Opens the Selection task pane, which you can use to select objects, change their stacking order, or hide or show objects.
Crop	Allows you to clip off parts of an image. Click the tool to activate it and then drag from an edge or a corner to remove a portion of it. Then click the Crop button again to apply the change.

The Format Picture task pane

You can also modify your images by using the Format Picture task pane. There are several commands that open the Format Picture task pane, but you can always right-click an image and choose Format Picture to open the Format Picture task pane, which displays several formatting options that are available for the selected object.

Do it!

B-2:   Adjusting pictures

Here's how	Here's why
1 Verify that the Web site picture is selected	
2 On the Format tab, click **Corrections**	(In the Adjust group.) To open the Corrections gallery.
Point to each preset	(In the gallery.) To see a Live Preview of the various effects.
Under Sharpen/Soften, click **Sharpen: 25%**	(The fourth option in the top row.) To increase the sharpness of the image by 25%.
3 Open the Corrections gallery	
Under Brightness/Contrast, point to a few options	To preview the effect of various brightness and contrast settings. (Many image style options are not practical for some images.)
4 Choose **Picture Corrections Options...**	To open the Format Picture task pane. You'll apply a custom picture correction.
5 In the Sharpness box, change the value to **10%**	(You can enter 10 in the box or move the slider to the left.) To reduce the Sharpen value to 10%.
Change the Contrast to **20%**	
6 Close the Format Picture task pane	
7 Go to slide 1	You'll continue working with slide 2 later.

8 Rotate the bottle as shown	
9 Sharpen the image by 50%	Click Corrections and choose the far right option in the top row.
10 Save the presentation	

Arranging and grouping items

Explanation

You can arrange items on a slide so that they overlap one another to achieve a particular design or layout result. You can also group items to format them as a single item.

Controlling the stacking order of overlapping items

By default, newer items that you add to a slide appear in front of older items where they overlap. The order in which items overlap one another is called the *stacking order*. To modify the stacking order, select the item whose stacking order you want to change, and select an option from the Arrange group, which appears on several tabs.

You can click the Bring Forward or Send Backward buttons to move an object, or you can click either button's arrow to display a list with additional options for adjusting the stacking order.

Grouping items

If you want multiple items to maintain their positions relative to one another, you can group them into a single object. This way, you can select them as a single item and move them or apply formatting. To group items, select them, click the Group button, and choose Group. You can ungroup selected items by clicking the Group button and choosing Ungroup.

Do it!   **B-3:   Arranging and grouping items**

Here's how	Here's why
1 Go to slide 2	
2 Select the image	It currently overlaps the WordArt object.
On the Format tab, in the Arrange group, click **Send Backward**	To move the image backward in the stacking order. The WordArt text is now fully visible.
3 Select the WordArt object	Click the edge of the placeholder.
Change the font size to **48**	To increase the font size slightly.
4 Verify that the WordArt object is selected	
Press CTRL	
Click the Web site image	To select the image and the WordArt object simultaneously.
5 Observe the ribbon toolbar	There are now two Format tabs; the Drawing Tools | Format tab and the Picture Tools | Format tab. This is because and image and a WordArt object are selected.
6 On either Format tab, in the Arrange group, click [Group ▾]	To display the Group menu.
Choose **Group**	The Web site image and the WordArt object are selected as a single item.
7 Click [Group ▾] again	
Observe the menu	The only command available now is Ungroup. You could choose it to remove the grouping you just created.
8 Press the ← key four times	To move the group to the left on the slide. If you don't have arrow keys, drag the selection.
9 Save and close the presentation	

Unit summary: Graphics

Topic A

In this topic, you learned how to insert and edit **WordArt objects**. You learned how to **resize** and **rotate** WordArt, modify **WordArt styles**, and apply WordArt styles to normal text.

Topic B

In this topic, you learned how to **insert images** from your computer and from Office.com and Bing image search. You also learned how to use the image editing tools to **modify images** and apply a variety of **corrections** and **effects**. Finally, you learned how to control the **stacking order** of overlapping elements, and **group items** on a slide.

Review questions

1 True or false? To create WordArt, you need to start with a WordArt object.

2 True or false? You can insert images directly from the Internet, without having to exit PowerPoint?

3 Why might you want to compress your pictures?

4 True or false? Once you have applied formatting to an image, you can't change the image without also losing the formats you had applied.

5 How can you open the Format Pictures task pane without using the ribbon toolbar?

Independent practice activity

In this activity, you'll apply WordArt styles and you'll add and modify images.

The files for this activity are in Student Data folder **Unit 5\Unit summary**.

1 Open Image practice.

2 Save the presentation as **My Image practice**.

3 Select the text "Outlander Spices" and apply WordArt styles of your choice to it. (*Hint*: click the Drawing Tools | Format tab.)

4 Set the title font size to **60**.

5 Apply a different set of WordArt styles to the sub-title "Top Sellers", and make the text larger, but not as large as the "Outlander Spices" title text.

6 On slide 2, apply the same style you applied to the sub-title to the text "Bay Leaf".

7 Rotate and move the text as shown in Exhibit 5-4.

8 On slide 2, insert the **Bay Leaf** image from the current Unit summary folder. Move the image slightly to the right, and use the Corrections tool to increase the **brightness and contrast** slightly.

9 Send the image to the back of the stacking order so that the Bay Leaf text is visible, as shown in Exhibit 5-5.

10 On slide 3, apply the same WordArt styles and rotation to the title, and insert the **Black Pepper** image. Increase the **brightness and contrast** slightly, and send the image backward in the stacking order.

11 On slide 4, apply the same WordArt styles and rotation to the title, and insert the **Cinnamon** image. Send the image backward in the stacking order and increase the **sharpness** of the image slightly.

12 Save and close the presentation.

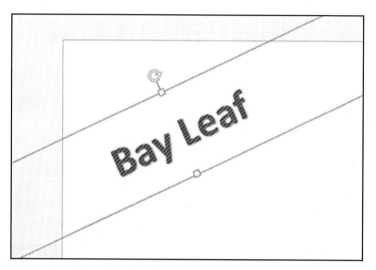

Exhibit 5-4: The slide 2 title, rotated and moved

Exhibit 5-5: The bay leaf image sent behind the Bay Leaf title text

Unit 6
Tables and charts

Complete this unit, and you'll know how to:

A Insert and modify tables, edit table content, control table formatting, and apply styles.

B Create, format, and modify charts.

C Create and modify SmartArt objects.

Topic A: Tables

This topic covers the following Microsoft Office Specialist exam objectives for PowerPoint 2013.

#	Objective
3.2	**Insert and Format Tables**
3.2.1	Create new tables
3.2.2	Modify number of rows and columns
3.2.3	Apply table styles

Explanation

You can add tables to a presentation to display data or to achieve a specific arrangement of content. A table consists of rows and columns. The intersection of a row and a column is called a *cell*. The cells of a table hold content; you can add text or numbers to a cell. Exhibit 6-1 shows a basic table structure.

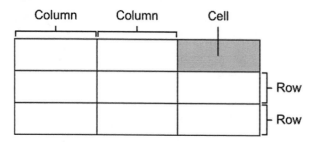

Exhibit 6-1: A basic table structure

Inserting tables

There are several ways to add tables to a presentation. If you're working with a slide layout that displays the Table icon, such as the Title and Content or the Two Content layouts, simply click the Table icon to open the Insert Table dialog box. Enter the number of columns and rows you want, and click OK.

Another way to open the Insert Table dialog box is to click Table on the Insert Tab and then choose Insert Table.

You can also use the Table menu directly to specify the number of rows and columns you want. Here's how:

1 Click the Insert tab.
2 Click Table to open the Table menu.
3 Point to indicate the number of rows and columns you want in the table; a Live Preview of the table appears on the slide for verification.
4 Click to add the table to the slide.

Another way to create a table is to draw it. Here's how:

1 On the Insert tab, click Table.
2 Choose Draw Table.
3 Drag on the slide to draw the table. This creates the table boundary.
4 On the Table Tools | Layout tab, use the buttons in the Rows & Columns group to add rows and columns to the table.

The Table Tools tabs

After you add a table to a slide, the Table Tools tabs appear. The Design tab contains style and formatting options, and the Layout tab contains tools for building the table and controlling spacing, margins, and other formatting options.

Adding content to tables

You add text and images to a table by entering the content in a particular cell. You can move from one cell to another by pressing the Tab key, or by using the arrow keys, or by clicking a cell. To add text content to a cell, place the insertion point in the cell and begin typing.

Do it!

A-1: Inserting a table

The files for this activity are in Student Data folder **Unit 6\Topic A**.

Here's how	Here's why
1 Open Announcement	(From the current topic folder.) You'll insert a table into this presentation.
Save the presentation as **My Announcement**	
2 Insert a new slide 4 with the Title and Content layout	(Select slide 3 and then insert the slide, or insert the slide and drag it to the slide 4 position.) You'll add a table to the presentation.
3 In the title placeholder, type **Projected Online Sales**	
4 In the content placeholder, click the Table icon, as shown	 To open the Insert Table dialog box.
Observe the Insert Table dialog box	 You can specify the number of columns and rows in the table.

5	In the Number of columns box, enter **2**	(Select the existing value and enter 2, or use the spin controls to set the values.) To insert a two-column, four-row table.
	In the Number of rows box, enter **4** and click **OK**	A table appears on the slide. By default, it has a blue color scheme. The Table Tools | Design tab is active.
6	Observe the Table Tools tabs	There are two tabs, Design and Layout. The Design tab is active by default. It contains commands and options for design-related tasks.
	Click the **Layout** tab	It contains commands and options for table layout-related tasks.
7	Type **2014**	To add the content to the first table cell.
8	Press (TAB)	To move to the next cell in the table.
	Observe the cell	The insertion point appears in the cell, indicating that you can add text to it.
9	Type **Projected Online Sales**	
	Press (TAB)	To place the insertion point in the first cell of the second row.
10	Type **1st Quarter**	
11	Complete the table as shown	

2014	Projected Online Sales
1st quarter	$100,000
2nd quarter	$120,000
3rd quarter	$150,000

12	Press (TAB)	To add a new row. When you're in the last cell in a table and you press Tab, a new row is created.
13	Type **4th Quarter** and move to the next cell	
	Type **$175,000**	
14	Save the presentation	

Modifying tables

When you're working with a table, you might have to increase or decrease the height and width of a row or column to fit your content or to achieve a particular look and feel. You can do this by dragging the row or column boundaries. If you need to insert a new row or column, use the commands in the Rows & Columns group on the Table Tools | Layout tab. The following table describes these commands:

Button	Description
Insert Above	Inserts a new row above the selected row.
Insert Below	Inserts a new row below the selected row.
Insert Left	Inserts a new column to the left of the selected column.
Insert Right	Inserts a new column to the right of the selected column.

To delete a row or a column, select the row or column that you want to delete. In the Rows & Columns group, click Delete and choose Delete Columns or Delete Rows.

A-2:   Modifying a table

Here's how	Here's why
1 Observe the table width	Both columns are wider than is necessary to contain the data.
2 Point to the line separating the two columns, as shown	
	The pointer changes to indicate that you can drag to adjust the column width.
Drag the column boundary to the left, as shown	
	A dotted line indicates the new boundary.
Release the mouse button	
	The width of the second column increases, and the text in the first column fits better.
3 Point to the bottom of the first row, as shown	
	The pointer changes to indicate that you can drag to adjust the row height.
Drag downward slightly, as shown	
	To increase the height of the first row.

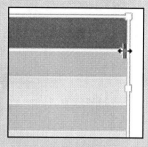

4	Point just inside the right edge of the table, as shown	
		You'll resize the right column without resizing the left column. (To resize the table so that both columns resize, you would drag from the right sizing handle.)
	Drag to the left to create the table width shown	

2014	Projected Online Sales
1st quarter	$100,000
2nd quarter	$120,000
3rd quarter	$150,000
4th quarter	$175,000

To reduce the size of the second column and the entire table.

5	Click in the last cell	If necessary, to place the insertion point.
	Verify that the Table Tools | Layout tab is active	(If it's not, click it.) You'll add a row above the last row.
6	Click **Insert Above**	(In the Rows & Columns group.) To insert a row above the current row. You don't want the new row here, so you'll delete it.
	Click **Delete** and choose **Delete Rows**	(In the Rows & Columns group.) To remove the row you just inserted. The first cell in the last row is now selected.
7	Click in the last cell	To place the insertion point.
	Click **Insert Below**	(Or press Tab.) To add a row at the bottom of the table.
8	Add the text in the last row, as shown	

2014	Projected Online Sales
1st quarter	$100,000
2nd quarter	$120,000
3rd quarter	$150,000
4th quarter	$175,000
TOTAL	$545,000

9 Save the presentation

Formatting tables

Before you apply styles and other formatting, first select the part of the table you want to format. The following table describes three selection techniques that you can use with tables.

To select a...	Pointer shape
Table: Click anywhere in a table to select the table and activate the Table Tools | Design and Table Tools | Layout tabs. When you point to a selected table, the pointer changes to include a four-headed arrow, indicating that you can drag to move the table.	
Row: Point just outside the table on the left or right side, and the pointer changes to a black arrow. Click to select the row, or drag to select multiple rows.	
Column: Point just outside the table on the top or bottom, and the pointer changes to a black arrow. Click to select the column, or drag to select multiple columns.	

Aligning text in a cell

You can control the horizontal and vertical alignment of text within a table cell. First select the desired cell(s), row(s), or columns(s). In the Alignment group on the Table Tools \| Layout tab, click the appropriate button. The following table describes the alignment buttons.

Button Name	Description
Align Left	Aligns the text to the left side of the cell.
Align Right	Aligns the text to the right side of the cell.
Center	Aligns the text equally between the left and right edges of the cell.
Align Top	Aligns the text to the top of the cell.
Center Vertically	Aligns the text equally between the top and bottom edges of the cell.
Align Bottom	Aligns the text to the bottom of the cell.

You can also use the options in the Alignment group to change text orientation in a cell. In the Alignment group, click Text Direction and choose an option. For example, you can rotate text 90 degrees to achieve a specific design effect.

The Table Tools | Design tab

You can use the Table Tools | Design tab to apply styles, shading, borders, and other formatting options. In the Table Style Options group, check the desired style options and clear the ones you don't want. The changes are applied to the selected table immediately.

In the Table Styles group, point to a style to preview it on the slide, and click to apply it. You can also use the Shading, Borders, and Effects buttons to change colors and apply other formatting.

Do it!   **A-3:   Formatting a table**

Here's how	Here's why
1 Point above the right column, as shown	**Projected Online Sales** $100,000
Click once	To select the column.
2 Click the **Layout** tab	If necessary.
3 Click ▤	(The Center button is in the Alignment group.) To center the text in the column.
4 Point as shown	2014
Click once	To select the row.
5 Click ▤	(The Center Vertically button is in the Alignment group.) To center the text between the top and bottom edges of the row.
6 Under Table Tools, click the **Design** tab	To view the design commands and options.
7 Check **Total Row**	(In the Table Style Options group.) To change the formatting of the Total row.
Check **Last Column**	☑ Header Row ☐ First Column ☑ Total Row ☑ Last Column ☑ Banded Rows ☐ Banded Columns Table Style Options
	To apply special formatting to the last column in the table.
8 Click the red color theme	(In the Table Styles group.) To apply a new table style.

9	Click **Effects**	(In the Table Styles group.) To open the Table Effects menu.
	Point to **Shadow**	To open the Shadow gallery.
	Select **Offset Diagonal Bottom Right,** as shown	

		To apply a shadow effect to the table.
10	Select the table	(Click an edge of the table.) If necessary.
	Drag the table to the center of the slide	It doesn't have to be exact.
11	Deselect the table	(Press Esc or click a blank area on the slide.) To view the finished table.
12	Save and close the presentation	

Cell fill options

Explanation You can fill table cells with a solid color, a picture, a gradient, or a texture. A cell fill applies to the cell background, behind any content in the cell. You can add cell fills by using the Shading list on the Table Tools | Design tab.

To set a cell fill, select the cell or cells you want to fill. Then, click the Shading button select a fill type. For example, to add an image to a table cell, choose Picture. In the Insert Picture dialog box, select a picture and click Insert. The picture fits to the cell's dimensions, and you can still add text in the cell; the image will be in the background.

Do it!

A-4:   Adding images to a table

The files for this activity are in Student Data folder **Unit 6\Topic A**.

Here's how	Here's why
1 Open Spice pricing	In the current topic folder.
Save the presentation as **My Spice pricing**	
2 Go to slide 2	You'll add images to the cells in the first column.
3 Click in the cell below "Spice image"	Next to "Cinnamon."
4 Click the **Design** tab	Under Table Tools.
5 Click **Shading**	In the Table Styles group.
Choose **Picture…**	To open the Insert Pictures screen. From here, you can insert images from your computer or from Office.com or a Bing image search.
6 Click **Browse**	To open the Insert Picture dialog box.
Navigate to the current topic folder	(Unit 6\Topic A.) You'll insert a picture from this folder.
7 Double-click **Cinnamon**	To insert the cinnamon image.
8 Press ⬇	To move the insertion point to the cell below the cinnamon image.
9 Insert the **Black Pepper** image	Click Shading and choose Picture, click Browse, and insert the image.
10 In the cell below, insert the Nutmeg image	
11 Save and close the presentation	

Topic B: Charts

This topic covers the following Microsoft Office Specialist exam objectives for PowerPoint 2013.

#	Objective
3.3	**Insert and Format Charts**
3.3.1	Create and modify chart styles
3.3.2	Insert charts
3.3.3	Modify chart type
3.3.4	Add legends to charts

Explanation

Charts are graphical representations of numerical data. PowerPoint includes several chart types you can choose from and you can modify styles and formats the same as you would other shapes and slide elements.

Working with charts

There are two methods you can use to create a chart: click the Insert Chart icon on a content slide layout, or click the Chart button in the Illustrations group on the Insert tab. Both methods open the Insert Chart dialog box. In this dialog box, select a chart type in the left pane. In the right pane, select the specific chart you want to create, and click OK. The chart is added to the slide and a Microsoft Excel spreadsheet opens with default sales data.

Charts require data, so this default spreadsheet content is required. You can then change the data and text for your purposes.

Do it!

B-1: Creating a chart and adding data

The files for this activity are in Student Data folder **Unit 6\Topic B**.

Here's how	Here's why
1 Open Site launch Save the presentation as **My Site launch**	From the current topic folder.
2 At the end of the presentation, insert a new slide	Use the Title and Content layout.
3 In the title placeholder, type **Comparison Chart**	
4 Click the Chart icon, as shown	 To open the Insert Chart dialog box.

5 In the left pane, select **Pie**	To view the available Pie charts.
Select the first pie chart, as shown	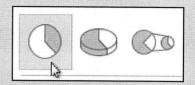
Click **OK**	Microsoft Excel 2013 starts, and appears alongside the PowerPoint window. Charts require data, so a simple spreadsheet with default sales data is displayed. This is not related to the table in the other slide.
6 In the Excel window, click as shown	

To select the cell.

Type **Projected Sales**	To modify the heading.
Press (↵ ENTER)	To select the cell below.
7 Type **$100**	This represents the $100,000 of revenue that the redesigned Web site is projected to produce in the first quarter. The pie chart is updated with the new data immediately.
Press (↵ ENTER)	To select the next cell below.
8 Type **$120**	To specify the value projected for the second quarter sales. The pie chart changes again to reflect the new data.
Press (↵ ENTER) and type **$150**	
Press (↵ ENTER) and type **$175**	
9 Click cell **1A**, as shown	

(To select the cell.) Make sure you don't select a cell other than one of the cells that has text or numbers in it.

10 Observe the chart	(In the PowerPoint window.) The pie chart has four slices, plus a legend that identifies what each color represents.
11 Close the Excel window	(Click the Close button.) To return to PowerPoint.
12 Save the presentation	

Changing the chart type

Explanation

To change a chart to a new chart type, click the Chart Tools | Design tab and click Change Chart Type. In the Change Chart Type dialog box, specify a new chart type and click OK. You can also modify specific aspects of a chart, such as the color of an individual chart component or the location of the chart legend relative to the chart.

Do it!

B-2: Applying a new chart type

Here's how	Here's why
1 Verify that the chart is selected	On the slide.
Under Chart Tools, click the **Design** tab	(If necessary.) You'll change the chart type.
2 Click **Change Chart Type**	(In the Type group.) To open the Change Chart Type dialog box.
3 Click as shown	
	To select the 3-D pie chart style.
Observe the Chart Styles group	Several 3-D chart styles are displayed.
4 Click **Style 3**, as shown	
	To apply a new 3-D chart style that shows the percentage values on each pie slice.
5 Click **Style 4**	(In the Chart Styles group.) To apply a lighter style. The percentage values that were part of the Chart 3 style are included in the style.
6 Save the presentation	

Formatting charts

PowerPoint 2013 includes new tools that make it easier than ever to format your charts to make them engaging and easy to comprehend. You can format individual chart elements or an entire chart.

Chart tools

When a chart is selected, the Chart Tools | Design tab and the Chart Tools | Format tabs appear on the ribbon toolbar. In addition to the commands and options on these tabs, three new tools appear next to a selected chart, as shown in Exhibit 6-2.

Click the Chart Elements button (the **+** symbol) to select whether you want a chart title, data labels, and a legend. Click the Chart Styles button (the paintbrush) to open a gallery of style and color options. Click the Chart Filters button to edit the data values.

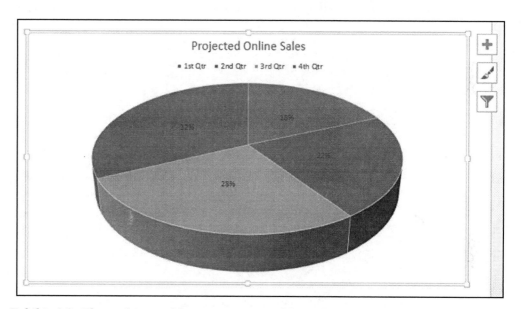

Exhibit 6-2: Three chart tool buttons appear on the right side of a selected chart

Applying a chart legend

Legends can be helpful to understand and track chart data. Not all chart types and styles include a legend by default. You can hide or show a legend, and you can change its position as needed. To add, remove, or position the chart legend, select the chart and click the Chart Elements button (the **+** symbol) to open a short menu. Point to Legend and click the arrow, and then select an option or choose More Options to open the Format Legend pane.

Applying chart labels

Labels can also be helpful to understand a chart. For example, it can be helpful to view numerical values that are represented by wedges on a pie chart. Some chart styles include labels, but you can always add or remove them as needed. To insert or modify chart labels, click the Chart Elements button (the **+** symbol) to open a short menu. Point to Data Labels, click the arrow, and then select an option. Or, choose More Options to open the Format Data Labels pane.

B-3:   Editing and formatting a chart

Here's how	Here's why
1 Click **Projected Sales**	(On the slide.) To select the placeholder.
Click **Projected Sales** again	 To place the insertion point in the placeholder.
Edit the text to read **Projected Online Sales**	
2 Click the edge of the chart frame	To deselect the chart title.
3 Click the Chart Styles button to the right of the chart, as shown	 Several chart style options are displayed in a scrollable gallery.
Click the first style	
Click the Chart Styles button again	To close the Chart Styles gallery.
4 Click the Chart Elements button, as shown	 A short menu appears; you can select or clear the options shown.
Clear **Legend**	To hide the legend.

5 Point to **Legend** and click the arrow, as shown

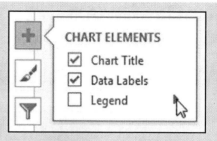

A menu appears.

Select **Top**   To display the legend at the top of the chart.

6 Observe the chart

Projected Online Sales

▪ 1st Qtr   ▪ 2nd Qtr   ▪ 3rd Qtr   ▪ 4th Qtr

The legend now appears above the chart.

7 In the pie chart, click an empty area in the bottom slice

(The 28% slice.) All slices are selected. You'll format an individual pie slice.

Click the same slice again   To select that slice individually.

8 Click the **Format** tab   Under Chart Tools.

Click **Shape Fill**

9 Select **Red, Accent 2, Lighter 80%**

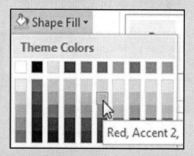

To change the slice color. The legend color is updated automatically.

10 Change the 32% slice to a lighter color of your choice

11 Save and close the presentation

Topic C: SmartArt

This topic covers the following Microsoft Office Specialist exam objectives for PowerPoint 2013.

#	Objective
3.4	**Insert and Format SmartArt**
3.4.1	Add shapes to SmartArt
3.4.2	Change color of SmartArt
3.4.3	Move text within SmartArt shapes
3.4.4	Reverse direction
3.4.5	Convert lists to SmartArt

Explanation

You can use SmartArt to create diagrams, such as organization charts, that represent relationships or processes and help you to convey information visually.

SmartArt diagrams

You can insert a diagram by using the Choose a SmartArt Graphic dialog box, shown in Exhibit 6-3. From this dialog box, you can choose from a variety of standard diagrams, such as organizational charts and cycle diagrams.

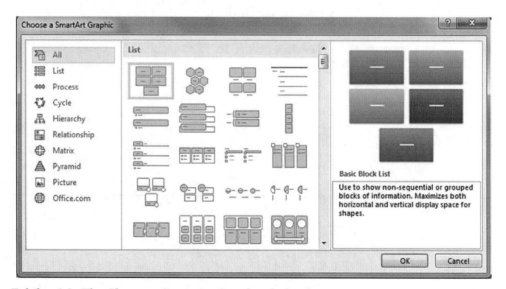

Exhibit 6-3: The Choose a SmartArt Graphic dialog box

There are seven diagram categories, which are described in the following table.

Diagram	Description
List	Shows non-sequential blocks of information, grouped blocks of information, or sequential steps in a task, process, or workflow. For example, you can use this diagram to show three sales teams that each contain several employees.
Process	Diagrams the steps leading toward a goal. For example, you can use this diagram to show the steps involved in hiring a new employee.
Cycle	Displays the steps of a cyclical process. For example, you can use this diagram to describe the process of developing a product, marketing it, and reinvesting profit in further research and development.
Hierarchy	Shows the hierarchical relationships among elements. For example, you can use a hierarchy chart to diagram an organization's management structure.
Relationship	Shows the relationships among items. For example, you can use a Venn diagram to show company resources used by two departments, differentiating among shared resources and resources used only in a given department.
Matrix	Shows the relationship of components to a whole, divided into quadrants. For example, you can use this diagram to display the names of four departments within a division.
Pyramid	Shows containment, foundation-based, hierarchical, interconnected, overlapping, or proportional relationships. For example, you can use this diagram to display the food groups, arranged from those you should eat often to those you should eat sparingly.

Creating an organization chart

You can display an organization's hierarchical details by creating an organization chart. You can create these and other types of diagrams by using SmartArt graphics. To insert an organization chart into a presentation, you can either insert a new content slide and click the SmartArt icon in the center of the slide, or click the SmartArt button on the Insert tab. Both methods open the Choose a SmartArt Graphic dialog box. In the left pane, select the chart type. In the right pane, select a specific chart, and click OK.

SmartArt Tools

When you insert a new SmartArt diagram, the Text Pane opens and the SmartArt Tools | Design tab is active. There is also a SmartArt Tools | Format tab that contains several style options that you can apply to your diagrams.

Adding text to a diagram

To add text to a diagram using the Text Pane, begin typing, or click to place the insertion point where you want to add text. The indent level of each item in the Text Pane corresponds to each item's position in the diagram. The further an item is indented in the Text Pane, the lower it appears in the diagram's hierarchy.

Using the Text Pane to add nodes to a diagram

The boxes that make up an organization chart and other types of diagrams are also called nodes; they contain the content for the diagram. To use the Text Pane to add a node to a diagram:

1 In the Text Pane, place the insertion point to the right of the item below which you want to add a new item. Press Enter to add another box at the same level.

2 Press Tab to demote the item so its box appears below the initial box in the chart.

3 Type to insert text in the new box.

You can promote an item by clicking its name in the Text Pane and pressing Shift+Tab. To demote an item, place the insertion point in the name and press Tab.

Modifying chart content and layout directly

You don't have to use the Text Pane to modify a chart's content and layout; you can work with the chart nodes directly. Select a node and type to add text, and use the buttons on the Design tab to add, promote, and demote items.

Do it!   ## C-1:   Creating an organization chart

The files for this activity are in Student Data folder **Unit 6\Topic C**.

Here's how	Here's why
1 Open Outlander site	From the current topic folder.
Save the presentation as **My Outlander site**	
2 After slide 5, insert a new slide using the Title Only layout	
3 In the title placeholder, enter **Web Site Launch Team**	You'll add a hierarchical diagram of the Outlander Spices organization.
4 On the Insert tab, click **SmartArt**	(In the Illustrations group.) To open the Choose a SmartArt Graphic dialog box.
In the left pane, select **Hierarchy**	To display the hierarchy options.
5 Select **Horizontal Organization Chart**, as shown	

Click **OK**	
6 Observe the SmartArt object	Two SmartArt Tools tabs appear on the ribbon toolbar. The Text Pane opens next to the SmartArt object so that you can enter text.

7	Verify that the insertion point is next to the first item	

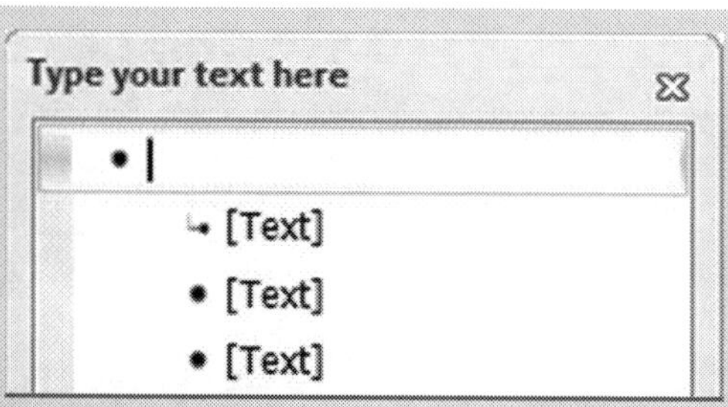

Type your text here ⊠

- |
  - ↳ [Text]
  - • [Text]
  - • [Text]

(In the Text Pane.) The text you enter here will be added to the first box in the hierarchy.

8	Type **Kathy Sinclair, President**	Kathy will lead this project. Notice that the text size changes automatically so that it fits in the diagram text box.

9	Click the next bullet

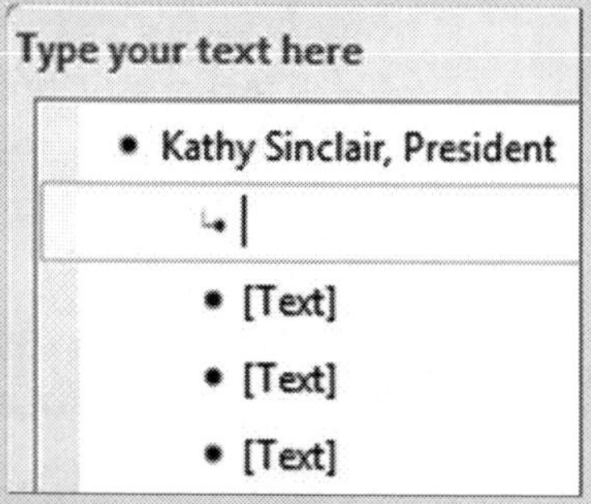

Type your text here

- • Kathy Sinclair, President
  - ↳ |
  - • [Text]
  - • [Text]
  - • [Text]

To place the insertion point in it.

	Add the other items shown

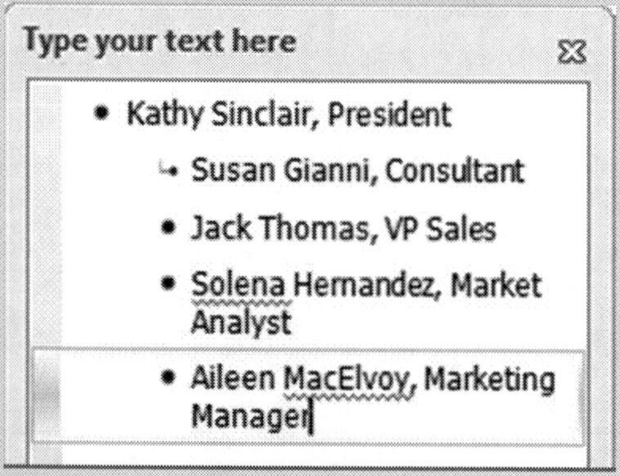

Type your text here ⊠

- • Kathy Sinclair, President
  - ↳ Susan Gianni, Consultant
  - • Jack Thomas, VP Sales
  - • Solena Hernandez, Market Analyst
  - • Aileen MacElvoy, Marketing Manager

10	Click **Text Pane**	(In the Create Graphic group.) To hide the Text Pane. The information is displayed in each node on the chart.
11	Save the presentation	Next, you'll customize the diagram.

Modifying diagrams

Explanation

After you've inserted a diagram and added some content, you can use a variety of tools to apply additional styles and formatting options that help you convey your information.

Customizing diagram layout and styles

The SmartArt Tools | Design tab contains several tools to help you arrange and format your diagrams. For example, to add a shape to a SmartArt graphic, click Add Shape no the Design tab and select an option. You can remove a shape from a SmartArt graphic by selecting the shape and pressing Delete.

To quickly format a SmartArt object, select the diagram and then click a style in the SmartArt Styles gallery. You can also customize a SmartArt graphic's theme colors by selecting an option from the Change Colors gallery on the Design tab.

You can also use the tools on the SmartArt Tools | Format tab to modify shapes, apply shape styles, fills, outlines and effects, as well as apply WordArt styles and align, group, and rotate items.

Reversing the orientation of a diagram

You can flip a SmartArt graphic to reverse its orientation. To flip a graphic, click the SmartArt Tools | Design tab, and click Right to Left. Click the same button again to return the graphic to its original orientation.

Do it!

C-2:   Customizing a diagram

Here's how	Here's why
1 Click the **Format** tab	(Under SmartArt Tools.) You'll increase the size of each box, apply a new style, and modify the formatting.
2 Click the edge of the first box	To select it.
Press CTRL	Now you can click anywhere in the other boxes to select them.
Click any part of the other boxes	To select them all.

3 Verify that all boxes are selected, as shown

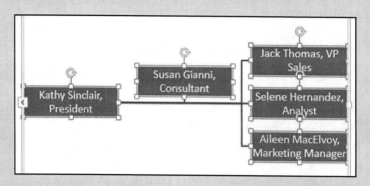

4 Click **Change Shape**	(In the Shapes group.) To open a gallery of shapes.
Select the rounded rectangle, as shown	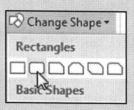
Press (ESC)	To deselect the boxes and observe the new rounded rectangles. You can change all the nodes in a diagram or individual nodes.
5 Click the **Design** tab	Under SmartArt Tools.
6 Click the More button	(In the Layouts group.) To display the Layouts gallery.
Click the **Organization Chart** layout	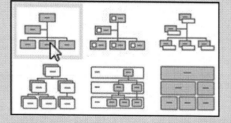
	To apply a new layout to the diagram. When you apply a new layout, previous shape modifications are not retained.
7 Click an empty area of the diagram	To select the diagram.
Drag the right-middle sizing handle slightly to the right	(The middle sizing handle, not a corner.) To increase the size of the chart.
Drag the left-middle sizing handle slightly to the left	To increase the size a bit more.

8	Display the Text Pane	Click the Text Pane button.
9	Click **Susan Gianni**	(To select that node in the diagram.) Susan Gianni is a consultant to the project, reporting directly to Kathy Sinclair. While Kathy is leading the project, she wants Susan's daily communication to be with Jack Thomas.
	Click **Move Down** once	(In the Create Graphic group.) To move the consultant position down one place in the Text Pane.
10	Click **Demote**	(In the Create Graphic group.) To move the consultant box below Jack Thomas.
11	Hide the Text Pane	Click the X in the upper-right corner of the Text Pane, or click the Text Pane button.
12	Deselect the box and select the entire diagram	Click an empty area of the diagram.
	On the Design tab, open the SmartArt Styles gallery	Click the More button.
	Under 3D, click the **Polished** style	To change the style.
13	Click **Change Colors**	(In the SmartArt Styles group.) To open the Change Colors gallery.
	Under Accent 2, Select a style of your choice	
14	Click the box for **Aileen MacElvoy**	You'll add a new node under it.
	Click the **Add Shape** arrow	(In the Create Graphic group.) To open a menu.
	Choose **Add Shape Below**	To add a position that reports to Aileen MacElvoy.
15	Type **Matt Smith, Web Designer**	To add the name and title to the box.
16	Click **Right to Left**	(In the Create Graphic group.) To flip the chart. You can explore other styles and options until you achieve your desired results.
17	Save and close the presentation	

Unit summary: Tables and charts

Topic A   In this topic, you learned how to insert and modify **tables**, edit table content, **align** and **format tables**, apply **styles** and **fills**, and **insert images** in table cells.

Topic B   In this topic, you learned how to create and modify **charts**, change the **chart type**, apply **formatting** and **styles**, and use **legends** and chart **labels** to convey information effectively.

Topic C   In this topic, you learned how to work with **SmartArt objects**. You learned how to create an **organization chart**, edit its content, and modify the **layout** and **styles** of a SmartArt diagram.

Review questions

1 What is a table cell?

2 True or false? To add text to a SmartArt diagram, you have to work with the Text Pane.

3 What keyboard keys can you use to move from one cell to another in a table?

4 When the insertion point is in the last cell of the last row in a table and you press Tab, what happens?

5 True or false? If you create a chart and then decide you want to use a different chart style, you need to delete the chart and start over.

6 When you're working on a chart, how can you change the location of the legend?

Independent practice activity

In this activity, you'll create and modify a table, and create and modify an organization chart.

The files for this activity are in Student Data folder **Unit 6\Unit summary**.

1 Create a new, blank presentation with a Title and Content layout slide.

2 Type **Sales (in Dollars)** in the title placeholder.

3 Add a 6-column, 5-row table to the slide.

4 Complete the table shown in Exhibit 6-4.

5 Delete the last row and last column.

6 Resize the table and move it to the center of the slide. Apply styles of your choice, and compare the table to the one shown in Exhibit 6-5.

7 Add another slide using the Title and Content layout.

8 Type **The Project Team** in the title placeholder.

9 Insert a SmartArt organization chart and add the text shown in Exhibit 6-6. (*Hint:* Press Tab to indent an item, or press Shift+Tab to remove an indent.)

10 Apply styles of your choice and compare your chart to Exhibit 6-7.

11 Save the presentation as **My sales** and close it.

	1st Qtr	2nd Qtr	3rd Qtr	4th Qtr	
Cumin	30	45	45	30	
Thyme	50	80	80	60	
Oregano	85	60	60	75	

Exhibit 6-4: The sales table

	1st Qtr	2nd Qtr	3rd Qtr	4th Qtr
Cumin	30	45	45	30
Thyme	50	80	80	60
Oregano	85	60	60	75

Exhibit 6-5: The formatted sales table

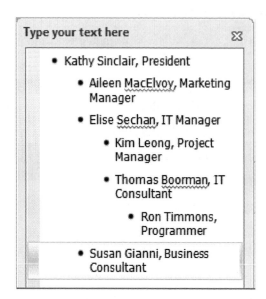

Exhibit 6-6: The organization chart content

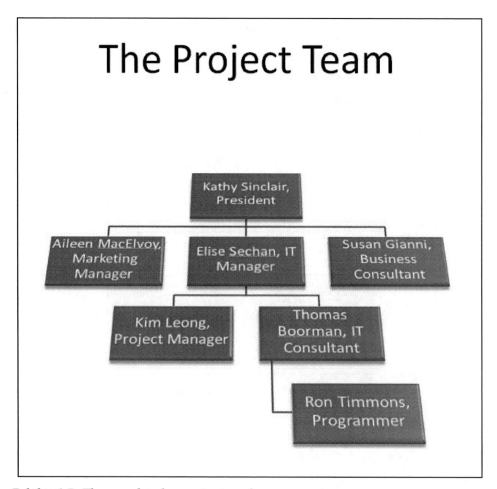

Exhibit 6-7: The completed organization chart

Unit 7

Preparing and printing presentations

Complete this unit, and you'll know how to:

A Proof a presentation by using Spell Check and AutoCorrect, and use the Thesaurus.

B Preview a presentation, hide selected slides for a specific audience, and rehearse using Presenter view.

C Print a presentation, a range of slides, an individual slide, handouts, notes pages, and the outline.

Topic A: Proofing presentations

This topic covers the following Microsoft Office Specialist exam objectives for PowerPoint 2013.

#	Objective
5.3	**Protect and Share Presentations**
5.3.2	Proof presentations

Explanation

When you're finished creating a presentation, you should use the spelling checker to ensure that it does not contain any spelling mistakes or typos. You can also use the AutoCorrect feature to correct your common mistakes as you type. You can also use the built-in thesaurus to help you find the exact word you're looking for.

Correcting typos and misspellings

When PowerPoint does not recognize a word, it's automatically underlined in red on the slide. You can correct spelling errors by using the Spelling task pane, shown in Exhibit 7-1, or by right-clicking an underlined word and choosing a replacement word. To open the Spelling pane, click the Review tab and click Spelling.

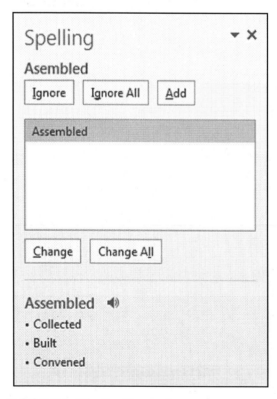

Exhibit 7-1: The Spelling task pane

Do it!

A-1:   Checking the spelling in a presentation

The files for this activity are in Student Data folder **Unit 7\Topic A**.

Here's how	Here's why
1 Open Product kickoff	From the current topic folder.
Save the presentation as **My Product kickoff**	
2 Click the **Review** tab	
Click **Spelling**	(In the Proofing group.) To open the Spelling task pane.
3 Observe the active slide	The fourth slide is active because it's the first slide with a misspelling. Words that are not in PowerPoint's dictionary are underlined in red, and the first incorrectly spelled word is highlighted.
Observe the Spelling task pane	It contains options to correct the spelling, as shown in Exhibit 7-1.
4 Click **Change**	(In the Spelling pane.) The misspelled word "Asembled" is changed to "Assembled," and the next misspelling is selected.
5 Click **Change**	To apply the correct spelling of "management." The next error is selected.
Click **Change**	To correct the spelling to "Preliminary."
Close the Spelling pane	
6 Right-click **Devloping** and choose **Developing**	To correct the misspelled word.
7 Press F7	To open the Spelling task pane again. The misspelled word "kickof" is selected.
Click **Change**	To correct the spelling of "Kickoff." A message appears, stating that the spelling check is complete.
Click **OK**	
8 Deselect the text	
9 Save the presentation	

AutoCorrect

Explanation

AutoCorrect automatically corrects any mistakes that you make as you type, as long as those mistakes are included in the AutoCorrect list. There are several built-in autocorrect items for commonly made mistakes, such as replacing "teh" with "the". You can use the AutoCorrect dialog box, shown in Exhibit 7-2, to add any words that you frequently misspell to accidentally mistype.

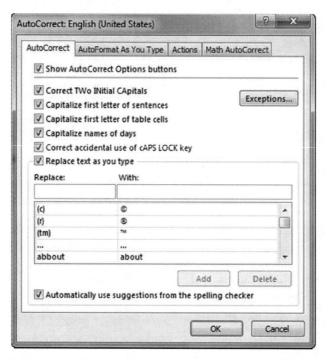

Exhibit 7-2: The AutoCorrect: English (U.S.) dialog box

Do it!

A-2:   Using AutoCorrect to proof a presentation

Here's how	Here's why
1 Click the **File** tab	To display the Backstage options.
At the bottom of the left pane, click **Options**	To open the PowerPoint Options dialog box.
2 In the left pane, click **Proofing**	To display the proofing options.
Click **AutoCorrect Options**	To open the AutoCorrect dialog box.
Observe the dialog box	The insertion point appears in the Replace box. By default, all options are selected.
3 In the Replace box, enter **outlaner**	To specify a word you often mistype.
In the With box, enter **Outlander**	To specify the correct word.
Click **Add**	To add the word to the AutoCorrect list.
4 Scroll through the list of the existing AutoCorrect items	Several commonly misspelled words are in the AutoCorrect list. You can use this dialog box to automatically correct the words you frequently misspell or mistype.
5 Click **OK**	To close the AutoCorrect dialog box.
6 Click **OK**	To close the PowerPoint Options dialog box.
7 Place the insertion point after **event**	(The last word in the last bullet on slide 5.) You'll add text here.
Press (↵ ENTER)	
8 Type **outlaner**	
Press (SPACEBAR)	The incorrect spelling is immediately corrected.
Type **cookbook**	To complete the bullet item.
9 Save the presentation	

The Thesaurus

Explanation

If you just can't find the right word, or if you need to verify the meaning of a word, you can use the Thesaurus. First, select the word you want to find an alternative for. Then, on the Review tab, click Thesaurus to open the Thesaurus task pane. A list of synonyms for the selected word is displayed. You can also press Shift+F7 to open the Thesaurus task pane.

Read through the list of options to find the word you're looking for. It also helps you to verify the meaning of a word and view the parts of speech that are relevant to that word. To replace the selected word, right-click the word you want and choose Insert.

Do it!

A-3: Using the Thesaurus

Here's how	Here's why
1 Go to slide 2	
Zoom out	If necessary to view the entire slide.
2 Select the word **inventory**	You'll replace this word with its synonym.
3 Click **Thesaurus**	(In the Proofing group.) To open the Thesaurus task pane.
Scroll down	In the Thesaurus task pane.
4 Right-click **stock**, as shown	
	You can also point to "stock" to display the arrow; then click the arrow and click Insert.
Choose **Insert**	The word "inventory" is replaced by "stock."
Press (SPACEBAR)	If necessary, to add a space between the words "stock" and "cost".
5 Close the task pane	
6 Save and close the presentation	

Topic B: Preparing a presentation

This topic covers the following Microsoft Office Specialist exam objectives for PowerPoint 2013.

#	Objective
1.5	**Configure and Present Slideshows**
1.5.5	Demonstrate how to use Presenter View
1.5.7	Annotate slideshows
2.1	**Insert and Format Slides**
2.1.3	Hide slides

Explanation

When a presentation is complete, you're ready to show it to your audience. Before you do, it's a good idea to preview it to ensure that the slide order is correct and that you want to include all of the slides for this particular audience. You can also record notes to remind you of key points you want to make, and you can use Presenter view to rehearse a presentation, allowing you to simulate the experience you'll have at show time.

Previewing a presentation

Slide Sorter view allows you to view several slides at once, giving you a rough preview of the overall presentation. You can also simply run a presentation to review it, or you can use Reading view. Reading allows you to view a presentation in full screen but also have access to the controls on the status bar.

To preview a presentation in Reading view, click the Reading View button on the status bar, or click Reading View on the View tab.

B-1:   Previewing a presentation

The files for this activity are in Student Data folder **Unit 7\Topic B**.

Here's how	Here's why
1 Open Kickoff meeting	From the current topic folder.
Save the presentation as **My Kickoff meeting**	
2 Switch to Slide Sorter view	
3 Select slide 4	
4 On the status bar, Click 🖵	To switch to Slide Show view. The slide show begins from the fourth slide. Notice that no presentation controls are displayed.
5 Press (SPACEBAR)	To go to the next slide in the presentation.
Press (ESC)	
6 Observe the window	The fifth slide is selected.
7 On the status bar, click 📖	To switch to Reading view. The slide show begins from the current slide and the status bar controls are displayed at the bottom of the window. The application controls are also visible at the top.
8 On the status bar, click the **Previous** icon	 To view the fourth slide.
9 Click **Previous** again	To view the third slide.
10 On the status bar, click the **Menu** icon, as shown	 To view the available commands.
Point to **Go to Slide**	To view all the slide titles in the menu.
Select the first slide	To go back to the beginning.
11 Save the presentation	

Hiding and unhiding slides

Explanation

When you create a presentation, you might to deliver it to more than one audience. In that case, you might want to include some slides for one audience that are not included for another audience. You can hide individual slides so they aren't included in the presentation, but they're not deleted from the presentation file so you can use them for another audience.

To hide a slide, select it and click the Slide Show tab. Then, in the Set Up group, click Hide Slide. The Hide Slide button works as a toggle; when you want to show a hidden slide again, you select that slide and click Hide Slide. Hidden slides are visible in both Normal and Slide Sorter views but they won't appear in the slide show.

Do it!

B-2: Hiding and unhiding a slide

Here's how	Here's why
1 Select the last slide	(In Slide Sorter view.) You'll hide this slide.
2 Click the **Slide Show** tab	
Click **Hide Slide**	(In the Set Up group.) To hide the selected slide.
Observe the slide	The number 5 has a line through it, indicating that it's currently hidden.
3 Run the presentation from the beginning	
Move through the presentation	The "Outstanding issues" slide does not appear in the slide show.
Exit the presentation	
4 Select the fifth slide	
Click **Hide Slide**	To unhide the slide.
5 Save the presentation	

Creating speaker notes

Explanation

In addition to your primary slide content, you can add speaker notes to your slides to use as a reference and to remind you of key thoughts you want to share.

Adding speaker notes

Each slide can include notes to help you remember key points in a presentation. You can use speaker notes for reference and you can print them to help you prepare for a presentation. Speaker notes are not displayed on screen during the slide show.

To add speaker notes to a slide:

1 In Normal view, select the slide to which you want to add notes.
2 Under the slide, click "Click to add notes."
3 Begin typing your notes.

You can also add speaker notes by using Notes Page view. Select the slide you want to notate, and on the View tab, click Notes Page. The page opens in a single slide view with a large text box beneath it. Click the text placeholder and begin typing your notes.

Do it!   **B-3:   Adding speaker notes**

The files for this activity are in Student Data folder **Unit 7\Topic B**.

Here's how	Here's why
1 Go to slide 1	
Switch to Normal view	
2 Click **Click to add notes**	(Below the slide.) You'll add notes to remind you of things to say during the presentation. If this placeholder text is not displayed, click Notes in the status bar.
Type **Tell the story of what got us here**	
3 Go to slide 4	
Add a note that reads **Special thanks to Sarah Watts**	To remind yourself to recognize Sarah Watts for her efforts.
4 On the View tab, click **Notes Page**	The slide appears with your note beneath it. This is how the page will look if you choose to print your presentation with the presenter notes.
5 Click the note text	To select the text placeholder and place the insertion point in it.
6 Zoom in on the text placeholder	(Use the view controls on the status bar.) To see the text better.
7 Add the text shown	You can add and modify notes in Notes Page view.

Special thanks to Sarah Watts and Bill Ott

8 Switch to Slide Sorter view	Notes are not displayed in this view.
9 Switch to Normal view	
10 Save the presentation	

Presenter view

Explanation

Presenter view allows you to separate what your audience sees from what you see, so that you can focus on delivering your presentation without having to turn your back to your audience to look at the public screen. This way, you have full control and visibility of the presentation; the audience sees the presentation as designed, while you view it on your computer along with controls and notes that only you can see.

Presenter view is the best way to rehearse a presentation because you'll be familiar with the Presenter view environment and you'll know what to expect.

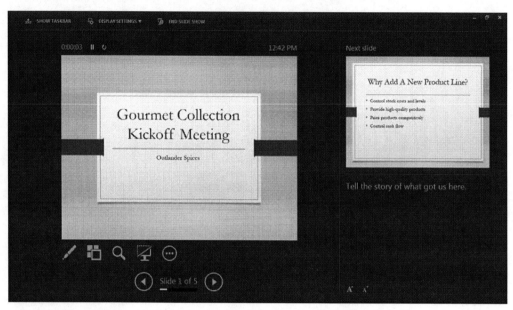

Exhibit 7-3: Presenter view

Rehearsing with Presenter view

To set up Presenter view, click the Slide Show tab and verify that Use Presenter view is selected. When you deliver the actual presentation, the audience will view a projection of the presentation and you'll use your computer's screen to control the presentation. You can rehearse the two-screen experience of delivering a presentation by pressing Alt+F5. This opens the presentation in Presenter view, as shown in Exhibit 7-3.

The main screen on the left shows what the audience sees, and the right pane shows the notes for the current slide and a preview of the next slide. A timer is displayed at the top of the window to show you the duration of the presentation, and several tools and navigation controls are displayed at the bottom.

Do it!

B-4: Exploring Presenter view

Here's how	Here's why
1 Go to slide 1	If necessary.
2 On the Slide Show tab, verify that Use Presenter view is selected	
3 Press (ALT) + (F5)	To open the presentation in Presenter view. The screen is divided into two views, as shown in Exhibit 7-3.
Explore the window	The main slide view shows what the audience sees. In the right pane are the notes for the current slide, and a preview of the next slide. At the bottom are navigation controls and other tools you can use. A timer at the top keeps track of the duration of your presentation.
4 Click the right arrow	To go to the next slide.
Observe the screen	The current slide is displayed, and "No Notes" appears in the notes section because there are no presenter notes for this slide. Slide 3 is visible under Next slide.
5 Navigate to slide 5	The preview shows a black screen and "End of slide show."
6 Press (ESC)	To exit Presenter view.
7 Save and close the presentation	

Topic C: Printing presentations

This topic covers the following Microsoft Office Specialist exam objectives for PowerPoint 2013.

#	Objective
1.3	**Customize Presentation Options and Views**
1.3.1	Change page setup options
1.3.2	Change to view in color/grayscale
1.4	**Configure Presentations to Print or Save**
1.4.1	Set handout print options
1.4.2	Print selections from presentations
1.4.5	Print presentations in grayscale
1.4.6	Print speaker notes

Explanation

By default, PowerPoint creates presentations in color. If you want to print a presentation without color, you can preview it to see how the colors and graphics will translate to grayscale or black and white. To preview a presentation in black and white or grayscale, click the View tab and click the corresponding option in the Color/Grayscale group.

Do it!

C-1: Previewing a presentation in grayscale

The files for this activity are in Student Data folder **Unit 7\Topic C**.

Here's how	Here's why
1 Open Outlander kickoff	From the current topic folder.
Save the file as **My Outlander kickoff**	
2 On the View tab, click **Black and White**	In the Color/Grayscale group.
3 Observe the slides	All colors are changed to black and white.
Observe the ribbon	The Black And White tab is displayed; it contains several options for customizing a black and white presentation.
4 Click **Back to Color View**	
5 On the View tab, click **Grayscale**	In grayscale, colors are replaced with varying shades of gray. This lets you preview how your presentation would print on a non-color printer, or if you choose to print without color.
6 Click **Back To Color View**	
7 Save the presentation	

Changing the slide size for print

Explanation

You can control the slide size and orientation for printing. In the Slide Size dialog box, *size* refers to the size of the slide on a printed page, and *orientation* refers to whether the pages are set up as portrait (tall) or landscape (wide). The default settings for a new presentation are for an on-screen slide show with landscape orientation. The slide numbering begins with 1. Handouts, outlines, and notes print in portrait orientation by default. You can change these settings.

To change the slide size and orientation for printing:

1 Click the Design tab.

2 Click Slide Size and choose Standard or Widescreen, or choose Custom Slide Size to open the Slide Size dialog box, shown in Exhibit 7-5.

3 From the "Slides sized for" list, select the desired format.

4 Select an orientation (Portrait or Landscape) for the slides and the notes, handouts, and outline.

5 Click OK.

Slide size options

The following table describes some of the size options you can use.

Format	Description
On-screen Show (4:3)	The default setting; used when designing a presentation that will be shown on screen. The slides are sized smaller than a standard sheet of paper. The "4:3" refers to the aspect ratio of your monitor; this is the standard ratio for older monitors.
Widescreen (16:9)	Used when designing a presentation that will be shown on a screen that uses the 16:9 standard (the international standard format of HDTV and many other modern devices).
On-screen Show (16:10)	Used when designing a presentation that will be shown on a screen that uses the 16:10 standard. (This aspect ratio is useful for displaying two full pages of text side by side.)
Letter Paper (8.5×11 in)	Prints the presentation on standard U.S. letter stock (8.5" × 11").
Ledger Paper (11×17 in)	Prints the presentation on standard U.S. ledger stock (11" × 17").
35mm Slides	Adapts the presentation for 35mm slides. (This setting is smaller than the default setting.)
Overhead	Prints your slides on overhead transparency stock (8.5" × 11").
Banner	Adjusts the slide size to create an 8" × 1" banner when printed.
Custom	Used to accommodate special sizing needs.

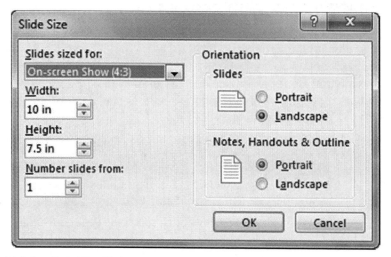

Exhibit 7-4: The Slide Size dialog box

Do it!

C-2: Modifying the slide size and orientation

Here's how	Here's why
1 Click the **Design** tab	
2 Click **Slide Size**	(In the Customize group.) To display a short menu.
Choose **Widescreen (16:9)**	To convert the presentation to a widescreen 16:9 aspect ratio.
3 Click **Slide Size** and choose **Custom Slide Size...**	To open the Slide Size dialog box. The current slide size is selected.
From the Slides sized for list, select **Letter Paper**	To prepare the presentation for printing on standard 8.5 x 11 inch paper.
Click **OK**	A dialog box appears.
4 Read the message	Whenever you go from a larger slide size to a smaller size, PowerPoint asks how you want to handle your content sizing.
Click **Ensure Fit**	
5 Open the Slide Size menu	The standard size is now in use because you chose the standard Letter Paper slide size.
6 Save the presentation	

Printing presentations

Explanation

To display the Print screen, shown in Exhibit 7-5, click the File tab and then click Print. You can specify the printer you'll use, the range of slides to print, the number of copies, and so on.

Exhibit 7-5: The Print screen

C-3: Printing a presentation

Here's how	Here's why
1 Click the **File** tab	To display the Backstage options.
Click **Print**	To display the print screen.
2 Observe the options	You can select the printer to use and set various print options.
3 Click **Print All Slides**	To open this options menu. You can choose to print only the current slide or a custom range of slides.
Click **Print All Slides** again	To close the menu.
Click **Print One Sided**	(If available.) To save paper, you can set it to print on both sides of the paper, and you can control whether the pages flip on the long edge or the short edge.
Close the menu	(Click Print One Sided again.)
4 Click **Collated**	When printing multiple copies of a presentation, use this list to specify whether the pages should be collated.
Close the menu	
5 Click **Color**	(To open the list.) Here, you can specify whether to print in color, grayscale, or pure black and white.
Close the menu	
6 Under Printer, click **Printer Properties**	To open the Properties dialog box for your specific printer. You can select other print options here.
Click **Cancel**	To close the dialog box without making any changes.
7 Observe the Copies option	You can enter a different number in the Copies box to print multiple copies of a presentation.
Point to the Print button	When you're ready to print, you'll click here.
8 Save the presentation	

Printing individual slides

Explanation

You can print an individual slide from a presentation. Here's how:

1 Select the slide you want to print.
2 On the File tab, click Print (or press Ctrl+P) to display the print options.
3 Under Settings, click Print All Slides to open a menu, and choose Print Current Slide.
4 Click Print.

You can also specify the number of copies of that slide that you want to print.

Do it!

C-4:   Printing an individual slide and a range of slides

Here's how	Here's why
1 Go back to Normal view	
2 Select slide 4	
3 Press ⟨CTRL⟩ + ⟨P⟩	To open the Print screen with the selected slide active.
4 Under Settings, click **Print All Slides**	To open the menu.
Select **Print Current Slide**	If you were ready to print, you would now click Print to print the one slide.
At the bottom of the screen observe the slide navigator	◄ 1 of 1 ► It reads "1 of 1" because there's only one page in this print job.
5 Under Settings, click **Print Current Slide**	
Select **Custom Range**	The insertion point appears in the Slides box below the menu.
Type **2-4** and then click in the preview area	Don't press Enter.
Observe the slide navigator	◄ 1 of 3 ► (At the bottom of the print preview screen.) The navigator now reads "1 of 3" because you selected a range of 3 slides.
6 Click the right arrow	To preview slide 2.
Preview slide 3	

7 Change the settings to print all slides	Under Settings, open the menu and choose Print All Slides.
8 Save the presentation	

Print output options

Explanation

PowerPoint provides several print output options. You can print slides, handouts, speaker notes, or the presentation outline.

Printing handouts

When printing handouts for your presentation, you can print them with one, two, three, four, six, or nine slides per page. When you're deciding how many slides to include per page, consider the readability of the handout. If you include too many slides with text, the handouts might be difficult to read.

To print handouts:

1 Click the File tab and click Print to display the print screen.
2 Under Settings, in the second list, select a handout layout.
3 (Optional) In the Slides box, enter the desired slide range. For example, you can print the speaker notes for slides 1, 2, 3, 4, and 7 by entering "1–4, 7".
4 Click Print.

Printing speaker notes

You can also print speaker notes for your presentation. Each page of speaker notes includes a small version of the associated slide. You can use these print outs to help you to prepare for your presentation.

To print speaker notes:

1 On the File tab, click Print.
2 Under Settings, in the second list, select Notes Pages.
3 (Optional) In the Slides box, enter the desired slide range.
4 Click Print.

Printing outlines

If you want to print only the text from your presentation slides, you can print the presentation outline. (This prints the text shown in the left pane in Outline view.) To print the presentation outline, open the Print screen. Under Settings, in the second list, select Outline, and click Print.

Do it!

C-5: Printing notes, handouts, and the outline

Here's how	Here's why
1 Open the Print screen	Press Ctrl+P.
2 Under Settings, click **Full Page Slides**	To open a menu.
At the top of the menu, choose **Notes Pages**	To print the slides along with the notes for reference and preparation.
3 Preview slide 2	(Click the right arrow on the slide navigator.) Even pages that do not contain notes will be printed with space at the bottom where notes would otherwise be.
4 Under Settings, click **Notes Pages**	To open the menu.
Choose **Outline**	The presentation outline is displayed in the preview pane. Printing a presentation outline can be helpful for preparation and review.
5 Under Settings, click **Outline** and choose **2 Slides**	To preview a handout consisting of 2 slides per page. This can be helpful if you want to conserve paper and reduce the number of handouts.
Observe the preview	There are two slides per page. Your notes are not displayed because they are typically not applicable to anyone but the presenter.
6 Save and close the presentation	

Unit summary: Preparing and printing presentations

Topic A   In this topic, you learned how to **correct typos** and **spelling errors** by using Spell Check, and you learned how to use **AutoCorrect** to create your own list of words that you frequently misspell or mistype. You also learned how to use the **Thesaurus** to replace a word with a synonym.

Topic B   In this topic, you learned how to **preview a presentation** in Reading view, and you learned how to **hide slides** for a particular audience. You also learned how to add **speaker notes** to help you during a presentation, and you learned how to rehearse a presentation by using **Presenter view**.

Topic C   In this topic, you learned how to prepare a presentation for **printing**. You learned how to preview a presentation in black and white and grayscale, and you learned how to control the print **output size** and **orientation**. Finally, you learned how to **print notes**, **handouts**, and the presentation **outline**.

Review questions

1 How can you correct a spelling error or typo? (Choose all that apply.)

   A Use the Spelling task pane.

   B Right-click anywhere on the slide and choose the correct word.

   C Use the Spelling and Grammar dialog box.

   D Right-click a word with a red underline and choose the correct word.

2 How can you customize the AutoCorrect feature?

3 How do you open the Thesaurus?

4 True or false? The audience can see speaker notes during a slide show.

5 How is Reading view different from running a slide show?

6 What is the keyboard shortcut for starting Presenter view?

7 What makes Presenter view the best way to prepare for a presentation?

8 What can you do if you want to print only the text from a presentation?

Independent practice activity

In this activity, you'll check a presentation for spelling errors, preview a presentation in Reading view and Presenter view, and prepare to print handouts for the presentation.

The files for this activity are in Student Data folder **Unit 7\Unit summary**.

1 Open Products.

2 Save the presentation as **My Products**.

3 Check the spelling of the entire presentation.

4 Preview the presentation in Reading view.

5 Preview the presentation in Presenter view. (*Hint*: Press Alt + F5.)

6 Prepare to print handouts, three slides per page. (Don't click Print.)

7 Save and close the presentation.

8 Close PowerPoint.

Appendix A

MOS exam objectives map

This appendix provides the following information:

A MOS 77-422 exam objectives for PowerPoint 2013 with references to corresponding coverage in ILT Series courseware.

Topic A: MOS exam objectives

Explanation

The following table lists the Microsoft Office Specialist (MOS) 77-422 exam objectives for PowerPoint 2013 and indicates where each objective is covered in conceptual explanations, hands-on activities, or both.

#	Objective	Course level	Conceptual information	Supporting activities
1.0	**Create and Manage Presentations**			
1.1	**Create a Presentation**			
1.1.1	Create blank presentations	Basic	Unit 2, Topic A	A-1
1.1.2	Create presentations use templates	Basic	Unit 2, Topic C	C-1
1.1.3	Import text files into presentations	Advanced	Unit 5, Topic A	A-1
1.1.4	Import Word document outlines into presentations	Advanced	Unit 5, Topic A	A-1
1.2	**Format a Presentation Using Slide Masters**			
1.2.1	Apply a slide master	Advanced	Unit 1, Topic A	A-6
1.2.2	Add new layouts	Advanced	Unit 1, Topic A	A-6
1.2.3	Modify existing layouts	Advanced	Unit 1, Topic A	A-3
1.2.4	Add background images	Advanced	Unit 1, Topic A	A-3
1.2.5	Control page numbers	Advanced	Unit 1, Topic A	A-2
1.2.6	Insert headers and footers	Advanced	Unit 1, Topic A	A-1
1.2.7	Modify presentation themes	Advanced	Unit 7, Topic B	B-1
1.3	**Customize Presentation Options and Views**			
1.3.1	Change page setup options	Basic	Unit 7, Topic C	C-2
1.3.2	Change to view in color/grayscale	Basic	Unit 7, Topic C	C-1
1.3.3	Demonstrate how to use views to navigate through presentations	Basic	Unit 1, Topic A	A-3
1.3.4	Modify presentation properties	Advanced	Unit 6, Topic A	
1.4	**Configure Presentations to Print or Save**			
1.4.1	Set handout print options	Basic	Unit 7, Topic C	C-5
1.4.2	Print selections from presentations	Basic	Unit 7, Topic C	C-4
1.4.3	Package presentations for CD	Advanced	Unit 6, Topic B	B-2
1.4.4	Save presentations as web pages	Advanced	Unit 6, Topic B	

#	Objective	Course level	Conceptual information	Supporting activities
1.4	**Configure Presentations to Print or Save (continued)**			
1.4.5	Print presentations in grayscale	Basic	Unit 7, Topic C	C-3
1.4.6	Print speaker notes	Basic	Unit 7, Topic C	C-5
1.4.7	Maintain backward compatibility	Basic	Unit 2, Topic A	A-5
1.5	**Configure and Present Slideshows**			
1.5.1	Create custom slideshows	Advanced	Unit 1, Topic C	C-3
1.5.2	Configure slideshow options	Advanced	Unit 1, Topic C	C-1
1.5.3	Rehearse timing	Advanced	Unit 1, Topic B	B-4
1.5.4	Configure slideshow resolution	Advanced	Unit 1, Topic C	
1.5.5	Demonstrate how to use Presenter View	Basic	Unit 7, Topic B	B-4
1.5.6	Navigate within slideshows	Basic	Unit 1, Topic A	A-1
1.5.7	Annotate slideshows	Basic	Unit 7, Topic B	B-3

2.0 Insert and Format Shapes and Slides

#	Objective	Course level	Conceptual information	Supporting activities
2.1	**Insert and Format Slides**			
2.1.1	Add slides layouts	Basic	Unit 2, Topic A	A-1
2.1.2	Duplicate existing slides	Basic	Unit 2, Topic B	B-3
2.1.3	Hide slides	Basic	Unit 7, Topic B	B-2
2.1.4	Delete slides	Basic	Unit 2, Topic B	B-3
2.1.5	Modify slide backgrounds	Advanced	Unit 7, Topic B	B-1
2.1.6	Apply styles to slides	Advanced	Unit 5, Topic A	A-1
2.2	**Insert and Format Shapes**			
2.2.1	Modify shape backgrounds	Basic	Unit 4, Topic B	B-1
2.2.2	Apply borders to shapes	Basic	Unit 4, Topic B	B-1
2.2.3	Resize shapes	Basic	Unit 4, Topic B	B-3
2.2.4	Insert shapes	Basic	Unit 4, Topic B	B-1
2.2.5	Create custom shapes	Basic	Unit 4, Topic A	A-2
2.2.6	Apply styles to shapes	Basic	Unit 4, Topic B	B-1

#	Objective	Course level	Conceptual information	Supporting activities
2.3	**Order and Group Shapes and Slides**			
2.3.1	Insert section headers	Advanced	Unit 1, Topic A	A-9
2.3.2	Modify slide order	Basic	Unit 2, Topic B	B-1
2.3.3	Align and group shapes	Basic	Unit 4, Topic B	B-2
2.3.4	Display gridlines	Basic	Unit 4, Topic B	B-5
3.0	**Create Slide Content**			
3.1	**Insert and Format Text**			
3.1.1	Change text to WordArt	Basic	Unit 5, Topic A	A-1
3.1.2	Create multiple columns in a single shape	Basic	Unit 4, Topic C	C-4
3.1.3	Insert hyperlinks	Advanced	Unit 5, Topic B	B-4
3.1.4	Apply formatting and styles to text	Basic	Unit 3, Topic A	A-1
3.1.5	Create bulleted and numbered lists	Basic	Unit 2, Topic A	A-3
3.2	**Insert and Format Tables**			
3.2.1	Create new tables	Basic	Unit 6, Topic A	A-1
3.2.2	Modify number of rows and columns	Basic	Unit 6, Topic A	A-1
3.2.3	Apply table styles	Advanced	Unit 3, Topic B	B-3
3.2.4	Import tables from external sources	Advanced	Unit 5, Topic B	B-1
3.3	**Insert and Format Charts**			
3.3.1	Create and modify chart styles	Basic	Unit 6, Topic B	B-2
3.3.2	Insert charts	Basic	Unit 6, Topic B	B-1
3.3.3	Modify chart type	Basic	Unit 6, Topic B	B-2
3.3.4	Add legends to charts	Basic	Unit 6, Topic B	B-3
3.3.5	Modify chart parameters	Advanced	Unit 3, Topic C	C-1
3.3.6	Import charts from external sources	Advanced	Unit 3, Topic C	

#	Objective	Course level	Conceptual information	Supporting activities
3.4	**Insert and Format SmartArt**			
3.4.1	Add shapes to SmartArt	Basic	Unit 6, Topic C	C-2
3.4.2	Change color of SmartArt	Basic	Unit 6, Topic C	C-2
3.4.3	Move text within SmartArt shapes	Basic	Unit 6, Topic C	C-2
3.4.4	Reverse direction	Basic	Unit 6, Topic C	C-2
3.4.5	Convert lists to SmartArt	Advanced	Unit 3, Topic A	A-1
3.5	**Insert and Format Images**			
3.5.1	Resize images	Advanced	Unit 2, Topic A	A-3
3.5.2	Crop images	Advanced	Unit 2, Topic A	A-1
3.5.3	Apply effects	Advanced	Unit 2, Topic A	A-2
3.5.4	Apply styles	Basic	Unit 5, Topic A	B-2
3.6	**Insert and Format Media**			
3.6.1	Adjust media window size	Advanced	Unit 2, Topic B	B-1
3.6.2	Trim timing on media clips	Advanced	Unit 2, Topic B	B-3
3.6.3	Set start/stop times	Advanced	Unit 2, Topic B	B-4
3.6.4	Set media options	Advanced	Unit 2, Topic B	B-2, B-3, B-4
3.6.5	Link to external media	Advanced	Unit 2, Topic B	

4.0 Apply Transitions and Animations

4.1 Apply Transitioning between Slides

#	Objective	Course level	Conceptual information	Supporting activities
4.1.1	Insert transitions between slides	Advanced	Unit 1, Topic B	B-1
4.1.2	Manage multiple transitions	Advanced	Unit 1, Topic B	B-1
4.1.3	Modify transition effect options	Advanced	Unit 1, Topic B	B-1

4.2 Animate Slide Content

#	Objective	Course level	Conceptual information	Supporting activities
4.2.1	Apply animations to shapes	Advanced	Unit 2, Topic C	C-1
4.2.2	Apply animations to text strings	Advanced	Unit 2, Topic C	C-1
4.2.3	Add paths to animations	Advanced	Unit 2, Topic C	
4.2.4	Modify animation options	Advanced	Unit 2, Topic C	C-1

#	Objective	Course level	Conceptual information	Supporting activities
4.3	**Set Timing for Transitions and Animations**			
4.3.1	Modify duration of effects	Advanced	Unit 1, Topic B	B-1
4.3.2	Configure start and finish options	Advanced	Unit 1, Topic B	B-3
4.3.3	Reorder animations	Advanced	Unit 2, Topic C	C-1
4.3.4	Demonstrate how to use the Animation Pane	Advanced	Unit 2, Topic C	C-1

5.0   Manage Multiple Presentations

5.1   Merge Content from Multiple Presentations

#	Objective	Course level	Conceptual information	Supporting activities
5.1.1	Merge multiple presentations	Advanced	Unit 6, Topic A	A-5
5.1.2	Reuse slides from other presentations	Basic	Unit 2, Topic B	B-4
5.1.3	View multiple presentations	Advanced	Unit 6, Topic A	A-5

5.2   Track Changes and Resolve Differences

#	Objective	Course level	Conceptual information	Supporting activities
5.2.1	Set track changes	Advanced	Unit 6, Topic A	A-5
5.2.2	Modify options for track changes	Advanced	Unit 6, Topic A	
5.2.3	Discard changes from specific users	Advanced	Unit 6, Topic A	A-5
5.2.4	Manage comments	Advanced	Unit 6, Topic A	A-1

5.3   Protect and Share Presentations

#	Objective	Course level	Conceptual information	Supporting activities
5.3.1	Encrypt presentations with a password	Advanced	Unit 6, Topic A	A-4
5.3.2	Proof presentations	Basic	Unit 7, Topic A	A-1
5.3.3	Mark as final	Advanced	Unit 6, Topic A	A-3
5.3.4	Compress media	Advanced	Unit 2, Topic B	B-3
5.3.5	Embed fonts	Advanced	Unit 6, Topic B	B-2
5.3.6	Restrict permissions	Advanced	Unit 6, Topic A	
5.3.7	Remove presentation metadata	Advanced	Unit 6, Topic A	A-3
5.3.8	Check for accessibility issues	Advanced	Unit 6, Topic A	A-3
5.3.9	Check for compatibility issues	Advanced	Unit 6, Topic A	A-3

Course summary

This summary contains information to help you bring the course to a successful conclusion. Using this information, you will be able to:

A Use the summary text to reinforce what you've learned in class.

B Determine the next course in this series, as well as any other resources that might help you continue to learn about PowerPoint 2013.

Topic A: Course summary

Use the following summary text to reinforce what you've learned in class.

Unit summaries

Unit 1

In this unit, you learned how to open a presentation, **start a slide show**, and navigate a presentation. You explored **Live Preview** and the **Backstage** options, and you identified components of the **PowerPoint interface**. You learned how to switch between Normal view, Outline view, Slide Sorter, Notes Page, and Reading view, and finally, you learned how to control the magnification by using the **Zoom controls**.

Unit 2

In this unit, you learned how to create a new, blank presentation, apply different **slide layout options**, **add slides**, **enter text** and **bulleted text**, and edit text on a slide. You learned how to move, resize, and delete **content placeholders**, **save** and update a presentation, ensure **backwards compatibility** for older versions of PowerPoint, **arrange**, **delete** and **duplicate** slides, create a presentation based on a **template**, and apply **design themes** to quickly change the look and feel of the presentation.

Unit 3

In this unit, you learned how to change the **font**, **size** and **color** of text, and use the **Format Painter** to repeat text formatting. You modified **bullet styles** and created a **numbered list**, and you **formatted paragraphs** by controlling **alignment**, **line spacing**, and **indentation**. You also learned how to **replace text** and **move and copy text** to other slides, and you learned how to use the **Clipboard pane** to copy and paste multiple items.

Unit 4

In this unit, you learned how to create and modify basic **shapes** and **lines**, **change a shape** to another shape, apply **shape styles**, apply **fill color** and **outline color**, **effects**, and create a **custom default shape**. You also learned how to **duplicate** and **move shapes**, **resize** and **rotate shapes**, **align shapes**, apply **text content** to shapes, **format text** in a shape, control text **orientation**, and create and format **text boxes**.

Unit 5

In this unit, you learned how to insert and edit **WordArt objects**, **resize** and **rotate** WordArt, modify **WordArt styles**, and apply WordArt styles to normal text. You also learned how to **insert images** from your computer and from Office.com and Bing image search, and use the image editing tools to **modify images** and apply a variety of **corrections** and **effects**. Finally, you learned how to control the **stacking order** of overlapping elements, and **group items** on a slide.

Unit 6

In this unit, you learned how to insert and modify **tables**, edit table content, **align** and **format tables**, apply **styles** and **fills**, and **insert images** in table cells. You also learned how to create and modify **charts**, change the **chart type**, apply **formatting** and **styles**, and use **legends** and chart **labels** to convey information effectively. You also learned how to work with **SmartArt objects**, create an **organization chart**, edit its content, and modify the **layout** and **styles** of a SmartArt diagram.

Unit 7

In this unit, you learned how to **correct typos** and **spelling errors** by using Spell Check, and you learned how to use **AutoCorrect** to create your own list of words that you frequently misspell or mistype. You also learned how to use the **Thesaurus** to replace a word with a synonym, **preview a presentation** in Reading view, and **hide slides** for a particular audience. You also learned how to add **speaker notes** and rehearse a presentation by using **Presenter view**. Finally, you learned how to prepare a presentation for **printing**, control the print **output size** and **orientation**, and **print notes**, **handouts**, and the presentation **outline**.

Topic B: Continued learning after class

It is impossible to learn how to use any software effectively in a single day. To get the most out of this class, you should begin working with PowerPoint to perform real tasks as soon as possible. We also offer resources for continued learning.

Next courses in this series

This is the first course in this series. The next course in this series is:

- *PowerPoint 2013: Advanced*

Other resources

For more information on this and other topics, go to **www.Crisp360.com**.

Crisp360 is an online community where you can expand your knowledge base, connect with other professionals, and purchase individual training solutions.

Glossary

AutoCorrect

A feature that automatically corrects typing mistakes you make if the mistakes are included in the AutoCorrect list.

Backstage view

The options displayed when you click the File tab; these commands are for taking action on a file, such as setting options, printing a file, and opening and saving presentations.

Cell

The intersection of a row and a column; content is contained in table cells.

Chart

A graphical representation of numerical data. PowerPoint includes several chart types and various formatting options you can use to modify them.

Clipboard

A temporary storage area that holds the text or object you have cut or copied until you specify where to place it in a document. The Windows Clipboard can hold only one selection at a time and is cleared when you shut down your computer.

Grid lines

A set of intersecting lines that appear on a slide to help you align content precisely.

Fill

A solid color, picture, gradient, or texture used as a shape background or a table cell background.

Live Preview

A feature that temporarily applies the setting or format you are pointing to in a list or gallery so you can see what the result will be.

Mini toolbar

A floating palette that appears immediately after you select text on a slide. The Mini toolbar contains some of the formatting options available in the Font and Paragraph groups.

Normal view

The default view in which developers usually work to create slides.

Paragraph formatting

Any formatting that can be applied to whole paragraphs (e.g. text alignment and line spacing).

Presenter view

A view that allows you to separate what your audience sees from what you see, so that you can focus on delivering your presentation without having to turn your back to your audience to look at the public screen.

Quick Access toolbar

A toolbar that contains icons for frequently used commands. Can be customized to include the commands you specify.

Reading view

A view that provides a full-screen view of a presentation, as in Slide Show view, but with the status bar and the Windows taskbar visible.

Ribbon

The toolbar that contains the primary tools and commands, divided among tabs and contextual tabs.

Slide Sorter view

Provides a miniature view of all slides in a presentation. You can change the order of slides in this view.

SmartArt

Pre-built and fully customizable objects you can use to create diagrams such as organization charts.

Speaker notes

Notes you can add to your slides to use as a reference and to remind you of key thoughts you want to share.

WordArt

A text object with predefined effects that you can fully customize.

Index